C000212429

CYC

TRAILS

OF

THE

YORKSHIRE

DALES

BY

DAVID JOHNSON

CASDEC LTD

Dedications

I would like to dedicate this book to my sister Iris and my brother in law Jack for having the patience to introduce me to the wonderful world of cycling all those years ago.

Acknowledgements

To my wife Doris for her endless patience in proof reading and correcting the numerous draft copies!

My sincere thanks to Alan Bell of Tamlyn music for allowing me to use an extract from his song "Alice White".

My thanks to my old mate Peter Dwyer for the loan of valuable photographic equipment.

Finally to my old pals Clive & Maureen Kristen for all their help and support in putting the book together.

Cycling Trails of the Yorkshire Dales

Published by Casdec Ltd
22 Harraton Terrace
Birtley
Chester-le-Street
Co. Durham
DH3 2QG

Tel: (091) 410 5556
Fax: (091) 410 0229

Written by David Johnson

First Published May 1994

© Casdec May 1994

All rights reserved. No part of this publication may be repro-
duced, stored in a retrieval system or transmitted in any form or by
any means, electronic, mechanical, photocopying, recording or
otherwise, without the prior consent of the copyright owners.

Views and opinions expressed in this book are those of the author
and are not to be attributed to the publishers.

ISBN - 0 907595 90 1

Cycle Trails Of The Dales

(veteran cyclist David Johnson invites you to join
him on his favourite rides)

Introduction

*H*i, I have put together a collection of my favourite rides in the
Yorkshire Dales, mainly centred around the Skipton, Otley,
Haworth and the East Lancs area, but in some cases going as far
as Hawes in Wensleydale and Ingleton at the foot of Kingdale.

Some of these rides I have been doing for the last 45 years. In
some cases because roads have become so crowded and not really
any longer pleasant to cycle on, I have chosen secondary roads
that follow the same direction or even ancient green roads. In all
cases this has led to a more pleasant day out and a greater sense of
freedom and enjoyment.

These trails are aimed at "occasional " bike riders. People of all
ages and both sexes who own a bike and would like to get out into
the Yorkshire Dales. Because of this I have given as much information as possible as to the difficulty of the rides. But then only
you can judge if you are capable of doing a particular trail. If in
doubt, do an easier one, or use your map to cut down the distance
on an existing one.

I hope that you can follow my maps and directions. I have thrown
in one or two true stories that have happened to me on these rides.

The rides are, wherever possible, circular and grouped in threes.
This means that you can usually do one big ride in a day or perhaps
do the three over a number of days, depending on how fit you feel.
I have tried to indicate just how difficult each ride is, from the
point of view of the hills on it.

These rides have been a pleasure to me throughout all of the
seasons of the year. Each time of year has its own particular

pleasures. But don't underestimate the weather in these areas. It can change very quickly. I have put in a page or two on what you might wear, eat and drink on the rides.

If you find yourself bowling along merrily, then you might have a strong tail wind behind you, do save some energy for the return trip into that same wind!

Magnificent Malham

Advice before Setting Off

*O*n these rides you should never be more than an hour from a cafe or shop selling food and drink. Even so I would always have something to eat in an emergency. Any kind of confectionery will do, my own choice is a Mars Bar. More importantly, do have a drink with you. If you do not already have one on your bike, invest in a bottle and carrier. Recent research has shown that we need to drink a good mouthful of fluid every 20 minutes or so when we are out on the bike. It does not matter if it is winter or summer. We lose just as much fluid in the winter when we have a lot of clothes on, as we do in the summer. If we don't drink enough then we lose a great deal of our energy. You can go a couple of hours on a bike without eating, but you need to drink every 20 minutes or so.

On these rides you will find many excellent spots to have a picnic. Why not take your own food and hot drinks with you for your main break?

An American, Two Germans And A Rowing Boat.

*W*hen I was cycle camping in Northern Scotland a few years back I stayed at a Youth Hostel in a place called Durness. Way out in the wilds of the Highlands. I got friendly with an American called Herb Mondrel. He was riding round Europe on his bike. As his family were of Italian descent besides having all his cycling gear, plus climbing gear! he also carried with him a huge, metal pan for cooking spaghetti in, "juusta like his Mother !" So that night in the hostel he cooked spaghetti for us both, plus a German violin player from a Berlin orchestra, called George and his girl-friend. I did the washing up!

Next day we decided to visit a peninsula called Cape Wrath. This is the most westerly spot in the U.K. mainland. The only way you can reach it is by rowing boat .

The man who rowed us over, had a Scottish berry on his head, and a half empty bottle of whisky in his hand. Well, it was Scotland, and it was at least 9.30 in the morning!

Being the only "native" of the U.K., it was my job to tell him where we wanted to go, and what time we would want meeting again. I made the mistake of telling him that George and the girl were German. He assumed, wrongly, like we all tend to, that they spoke no English. I can still see him looking at the poor girl, in her cycling shorts, and exclaiming in a broad Scottish brogue," Aye, she's got thighs like a stallion!".

We got onto Cape Wrath, and the point of this story! We all shared our food and drink together. If there are a few of you on one of these rides, this might be an idea for you to consider. The Dales are full of great picnic spots.

Some Ideas On What To Eat And Drink

*J*f you are going to do a lot of cycling, say on holiday, then you need to be aware of what you eat when you're not on the bike. Obviously the best diet is a balanced diet. But we'll have a look at the foods that effect cycling the most directly.

Carbohydrates are the best , you get them from foods like potatoes, bread, pasta, rice, pulses , vegetables and nuts. These are broken down by the body into glycogen, and used by the muscles. Too much though, and they're stored as fat! Remember the balanced diet, you need all of the essential vitamins and minerals to get the best from carbohydrates.

Sometimes on a bike we need a fast boost of energy. We get this from what are called simple carbohydrates. Sugar, confectionery, sweet foods and drinks. Other fast sources of energy, and better for you, are dried fruits, fruit cakes, biscuits and bananas.

Please don't forget about the need to drink on a very regular basis, summer and winter. A good mouthful every 20- 30 minutes. Do carry a bottle with you when you're on the trails, keep eating little bits so that you're never too hungry. Nowadays I have a lot of trouble getting my bike to ride past cafes. Thinking about it, I always did!

Getting Kitted Out : Clobber!

*T*he type of clothing you should wear on these rides is very much up to you. A lot will depend on when you do the rides. Especially the time of the year.

As a rule it is better to go for several layers of clothes, rather than for one good heavy article of clothing, as at you might if walking or hiking. You need to be able to adjust your clothing to meet your changing body temperature. Especially when you're walking up some of the hills in Nidderdale! This applies as much in the summer as it does in the winter.

One thing I never set out without, is what I call a racing cape. This is just a very lightweight jacket, without pockets, made of nylon, and weighs next to nothing and rolls into a very small pack that you can stick in your pocket. An old kagool would do just as well. I use it when I realise it is a bit colder than I thought it was. Because it is made of nylon or plastic, it keeps the wind out, and you quickly warm up. Of course you can use it as well for those annoying showers; yes it does rain in Yorkshire!

A lot of the new high tech. breathable materials have the advantage of being lightweight, warm and protect you from the rain. But don't worry if you're not into them yet. For our trails a lot of expensive gear is not necessary.

Braces may be out fashion, but for cycling they're ideal. Much better than tight elastic or a belt. On a bike you need to be able to breath in comfort!

Winter or summer I always have a thermal vest on. They keep you from getting chills and soak up any moisture. I usually have a short sleeved top on, but in the winter I also carry long knitted sleeves that you can pull over your arms(like leg warmers but for your arms).

In the winter, because of the chill factor, it is essential to have good warm gloves or mitts. Even in the summer I always wear a pair of mitts. They're handy if you fall off!

Helmets : To Wear Or Not To Wear.

*H*elmets are a tricky question. Let me say straight away that I always use one, cycling at home or on the continent. There are arguments for and against, I'll try to set them out for you. But the subject is both complex and controversial.

Do they prevent injuries? If there are no other vehicles involved, yes. If you're knocked off your bike by a motorised vehicle, then the evidence appears to be, not a lot! I make this point because some people think if they wear a helmet, then they don't have to be as careful.

In Australia where it is compulsory to wear a helmet when cycling, it has made no significant difference to injuries or accidents to cyclist, but the number of people using a bicycle has reduced by nearly 30%! But as I started off by saying, I wear one at all times on the bike, and so do most of my cycling mates. It's better to be safe than sorry for the bit of extra cost.

Tool Kit

*D*on't go mad and carry too much extra weight, but I always try to have the means of tightening or untightening every nut on the bike. I also carry a screwdriver, a puncture outfit and at least three spare inner tubes and tyre levers.

If you do have a puncture, then it's easier to change the inner tube than to mend the old one. One tip, I always carry a small amount of washing up liquid and a piece of clean rag. If you've had a bit of bother, then you can find some water, a puddle will do! and get your hands clean again.

I hope that these few ideas will enable you to get the most out of the Trails. If there is anything you feel that I should have mentioned and have not, then please let me know.

Lastly, one or two tips that I have found useful over the years. You will get a lot more enjoyment from your rides if you carry a good map. I was brought up on a Bartholomews half inch series, but that is no longer available. I suggest that you use an Ordnance Survey Outdoor Leisure Series Map. I have tried to give as much detail as possible, but do keep checking against your map. And never go down a hill unless you are certain it's the right way! You will, I hope, find interesting things to see and do that I have not mentioned. The Dales are full of interesting places, people, wildlife and spectacular scenery, enjoy your rides.

Contents

Trail 1	Dentdale Trail	Page 15
Trail 2	Lakeland Trail	Page 37
Trail 3	Haworth Trail	Page 65
Trail 4	Tea Pot Trail	Page 79
Glossary		Page 105
Addresses		Page 110

DENTDALE TRAILS

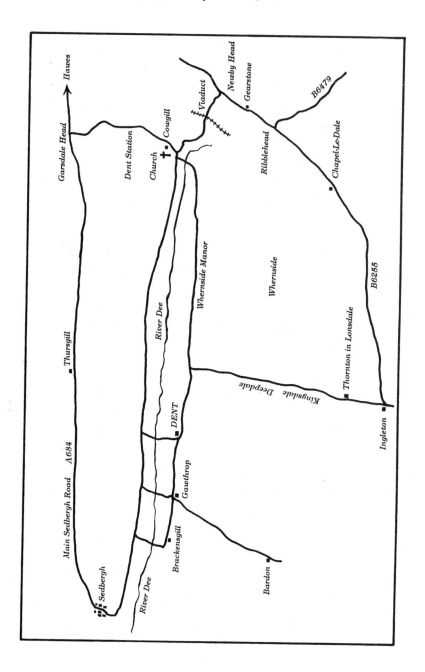

Trails Of Dentdale

*C*his is my favourite little area in the dales. In fact it's a Kingdom, or was anyway, with Dent as its capital. My favourite dale is Swaledale, but Dentdale is where most of my happiest times awheel have been spent in recent years.

These trails are essentially about the Yorkshire Dales, there is a rumour that Dent is in Cumbria! Rubbish! It's in The Yorkshire Dales National Park, so as any Yorkshire man will tell you, it must be in Yorkshire, common sense!

There is a lot to do and a lot to know in this magical little area. Where do you start? Well Dent has the highest railway station in England. Well over two thousand feet. If you want to walk to the station and you're in Dent Town, then set off early, it's 4 miles away in a place called Cowgill! Or wait till one of these trails take you through Cowgill and visit it then.

Many a housewife over the years has been proud of her fireplace, made from Dent Marble. Part of the floor in the church is, I believe, made from local marble as well. But perhaps most of all Dent is known for its "Terrible Knitters". This term was not a reflection on their ability as knitters, it meant that they were remarkable both for the quality and the quantity of the work produced. In the early nineteenth century this was a thriving local industry. Everyone in a family would knit. Men , women and children alike.

Making a living in this area has always been hard, but the locals are great, and have a very dry sense of humour, as this silly story shows:

"Ah's badly," complained Tom of Dentdale, mournfully. He took to his bed. His wife , Alice, looked solemn. "Tom", she asked him, "where dosta want ta be buried? "Ah dont want to be buried," he replied. "But if tha dees, Tom," insisted Alice, "thal ha ta bi buried." "Weel," replied Tom thoughtfully, "tak ma ta Conrnwall. I'd like ta bi buried bi t'sea." "Does ta think ah's made of brass," Alice

exclaimed indignantly. "Ah'll tak tha ta Dent, where tha come fra, and if tha doesn't settle theer, ah'll tak tha ta Cornwall!"

Anyway, on with the first trail, enjoy it. I really wish I was setting out with you.

St Andrew's Church, Dent

Trail 1
(Dent Town, Gawthrop, Brackensgill, Cowgill, Whernside Manor, Dent)

About 14 miles this one. It's the course of the Dent Run. This is an annual event, and I have been fortunate to run in it three times, including the inaugural run in 1984, held on the 24th of March. When I first ran it was described as a "fun" run. Most of us were fun runners with just a few club runners in among. You ran the full course,14 plus miles, and got a "time" for the half marathon distance, my time was 1 hour 40 minutes.

What's Up Doc?

The last time I ran the event was in 1986. By then it was a much more serious event. A lot of stretching , warming up and liberal applications of embrocation going on before the start. It was my custom to take my embrocation internally the night before! Anything up to a gallon, as my dear friends Clive and Maureen will confirm! I don't know if it makes you go any faster but it does numb the pain! and does not smell as bad as theirs!

I was 52 that year and running with my eldest son Paul who was 26. Funny that. When he was born I was 26years old,and of course 26 times as old as him. 26 years later I'm only twice as old as him! In what year do we meet? (Answers please to the editor in a plain brown envelope).

Back to the event. I still feel sorry for Paul. Anything can happen in an event of 14 miles plus and he had to contend with the unthinkable! his dad might catch him! Of course I didn't but I bet he was glad when he'd finished!

It was a rough day that year. Held in March as usual, it was very cold and after half way it started to snow heavily. The event was well organised, plenty of marshals, St John's Ambulance people and a mobile doctor. I remember the doctor because as the conditions deteriated she kept appearing at my side in a car. "What's your name, how old are you, where do you live?", the car would disappear and then ten minutes later reappear. The window would be wound down and the same questions asked "What's your name, how old are you, where do you live?" I suppose she was checking the older ones to see that mind and body were still in touch! That was typical of how well organised the event was.

The trail starts outside the village hall. Head out on the Sedbergh Road for half a mile and then take the left turn up to Gawthrop. This is a steep little hill but it's short and it's one of the few on this trail. Ignore the next left turn for Barbon you keep straight on. The little cafe and shop you have passed on your right is worth coming back to sometime. On a nice day you can sit outside on either side of the road. It was the favourite place for me and an old cycling mate called Bill Herron to stop. We solved a few of the worlds more serious problems there over a cup of tea, pity some of our leaders can't do the same!

The road narrows now and is not much more than a track. But it's quiet and peaceful as you head down to the side of the river Dee. Doris and I collect rosehips here in September to make rosehip syrup. You're also close to the home of The Rochdale Cowboy, Mike Harding. If you see a bespectacled hiker with a camera slung round his neck, and if he gives you a friendly greeting in a Lancashire accent, then it could well be Mike.

The River Dee, Dent

The track follows the side of the river for about half a mile until you come to the bridge. Cross over the bridge and then turn right at the T junction up the short hill. It's just about two miles now to where the next bridge would take you back over the river to Dent. Look carefully and you will see the start of the track along the east side of the river. Part of it is still cobbled and I suspect it is part of the old pack horse trail.

Three quarters of a mile and you come to the next bridge with Dent a quarter of a mile on your right. Carry straight on towards Cowgill, about four miles away. The road starts to climb up again and you have some good views of Whernside in front, and Deepdale on your right. On your right and across the river you can also see the road you will be returning to Dent on. What I remember best about this stretch of road is the smell of the wild garlic at the side of the road. Two or three good lung fulls on a warm day will certainly make your eyes water!

Just before the church at Cowgill you take the bridge over the river again as you start the return journey to Dent. This is one of the major feeding spots in the fun run. If you want to visit Dent Station then turn left just across the bridge and follow the track to Cowgill. A lovely half mile by the side of the river.

Crossing the River

Bath Time

Some years ago I was doing this walk with Gordon Hampshire and his sheepdog Keld. It was early spring and lambing time. Keld came running towards us and we both caught our breath in horror. He smelt like a poke of devils! Like other dogs he loved to roll in the afterbirth from the lambings. There was nothing for it, in the river he had to go. We were camping at Cowgill, and there is no way you could have a dog round the tents smelling like that!

It had been snowing and the river, besides being freezing cold, was also in spate. Getting him in was easy, Gordon, a well built lad, just grabbed his collar and slung him in! Getting him out was the problem! Before then I had never seen fear on the face of a dog, but that day as he struggled in the the freezing water, it was there to see! We finally got him onto the bank.

After he had shaken himself as only dogs can, Gordon stroked him and made a fuss of him. We had both panicked a bit as we struggled to get him out and were relieved it was over. It wasn't! He just set off and rolled in the same patch! In he went again, but this time we fastened some old rope to his collar.

Back to the trail, you turn right over the bridge and head back to Dent about four miles away. Take care on this narrow road. It gets so narrow that cars have trouble in passing each other. Apart from that it's usually quiet, peaceful with fantastic views all around.

A couple of miles before Dent you pass Whernside Manor. It is some kind of outdoor centre now, but tales are told that, in times past, imported slaves were kept locked in the cellars below!

Two or three short climbs and you are back in Dent on the cobbles again. Pass the old reading rooms on your right and then you're just yards from the beautiful old church. As you continue back to where you started from the Stone Close cafe is on the right, just after The Sun. Not only is the homemade food and drink excellent, they also play tranquil music, as you enjoy your tea. The cafe I mentioned at Gawthrop is also less than a mile away.

Sedgewick Memorial, Dent

Trail 2

(Dent, Sedbergh, Garsdale Head, Dent Station, Cowgill, Dent).

(About 24 miles in total).

*C*his is another pleasant and interesting trail you should enjoy. The countryside is varied and easily climbable most of the time. The exception is the first 3 miles out of Garsdale Head. Definately a walk and look round!

This trail starts from outside of the church by the Adam Sedgwick memorial fountain. The church is very old dating back to Norman times. Sitting in one of the old Jacobean oak pews, I always seem to get a feeling of what Dent must have been like long ago. The inside of the church has, to me a timeless aspect, perhaps the heart of Dent itself resides here. This feeling may stem from a few years ago when I visited the church and on display were the photographs of local men who had perished in the first Great War. God bless them, the faded photos were old, but the faces looked so young.

Old Year's Night And New Year's Day

As you make your way out of Dent you will pass the Sun Inn on your left and near by is the cottage of my friends Clive and Maureen. It's great on a cold winters night, to stagger out of The Sun, and be basking in the warmth of an open log fire in two tics!

The last leg of this trail will bring us back from Cowgill. This is the route I rode in on five successive old year's nights. I would leave my home in Bingley near Bradford about lunch time. Cycling up through Settle, Horton in Ribblesdale, Dent Head and down through Dent viaduct, Cowgill and on to Dent, about 50 odd miles in all.

It was usually getting dark as I cycled the last few miles. At the top of the last rise before Dent you get a lovely view of the old grammar school and the Church. Nothing on the roads usually, dusk settling in, and just the light of my cycle lamp for company.

Most years I was usually getting cold by now having descended from Dent Head. But I was warmed by the fact that I knew there would be a roaring log fire at Clive and Maureen's. As soon as I arrived Maureen would get a pot of tea going, and then time to stretch out in front of the fire with the two dogs,(two red setters), not Clive and Maureen!.

The Man With More Than A Handle To His Name

*O*ne year, before going over to The Sun around 10.30 to let in the New Year. We played the "adult" version of Trivial Pursuits. It's great fun just like the ordinary version. The difference is in the catergories. If I remember rightly they were, Orange, "sex and art in literature", Blue, "Facts of life", green, "jokes and rhymes", Yellow, "mythology", Brown, "famous uncovered", Pink, "hot times in history". I'm sure you get the general gist of it!

One of the questions from the yellow section, mythology, was "one of the ancient gods was called Priapus what was he famous for?" Anybody know? Well it turned out that he was the god of fertility. The statues of the day always showed him ready for action as you might say. It is even suggested by some leading authorities, that these statues were the early versions of the modern day hat stand! We shall probably never know.

Take the road out of Dent towards Sedbergh. After about three quarters of a mile you will come to the left fork for Gawthrop. Your road curves to the right down to the bridge over the river Dee. The next three or four miles to Sedbergh are some of my favourite ones either walking or cycling. There are more hedges than drystone walls and the area is pastoral with a very "lakeland" look to it.

The road follows the river on your left, gradually climbing up through the very pleasant, partly wooded slopes. The climbs are not very taxing and they give you fine views of the river and the valley below, on a spring day the colours are breathtaking. The final ascent before the town is quite steep and takes you onto a sharp left turn over the river. I often stop here and look over the bridge at the trout swimming below in the rock pools.

After the bridge you ride up to the next T junction. The beautiful old church of St Andrew is on your left and on your right is a favourite old book shop of mine. You turn right onto a cobbled street that takes you through the centre of this ancient market town. If you fancy a cuppa there are some nice cafes on this street.

The road winds to the left at the end of the cobbles and you are heading out on the Kirby Stephen road, but only for a hundred yards or so. Take the right hand road, A684 for Hawes as it follows the course of the river Clough.

The next five miles or so to Thursgill is a series of steady climbs. Nothing serious but often you are going into a head wind. Once through Thursgill you change direction as you start to climb gradually to Garsdale Head. The last five miles were spent in quite open country. Now you are in a much narrower valley. In my experience any previous strong winds are left behind. Just sit back, use a low gear,(a big sprocket on the back wheel), and keep peddling steadily.

At Garsdale Head, just a few railway cottages and a telephone box. Take the right fork to Dent Station and Cowgill. Walk for the first mile or so as it really is steep. All around you is the evidence of past efforts to wrench a living from this bleak area. Efforts to find coal and lead have left their traces all around you, in this scarred and battered landscape.

Once you are on the top the views are spectacular. Whernside to your front and left, The Howgill Fells to your right, and Dentdale spread out below you as you start to descend into the valley again. Take care as you pass Dent Station. The next half mile is steep! The road also bends and twists and the surface is not good, so keep your brakes on as you come to the next junction. The road goes straight forward over a bridge but you take the right fork for Dent, about four miles away. You will quickly pass Cowgill church on your right.

My cycling club, The Pennine C.C., has camped on John Irvins farm at Cowgill, for about 30 years non stop! John once told me about a sign in the church. I can't remember the exact words, but the message was "come inside now and then, so that when they carry you in for the last time, God will know who you are!". Seems fair enough!

A nice steady ride back to Dent now. The road follows the course of the river in a series of gentle climbs. The last half mile into Dent is the one I described earlier on, so look out for the views of the church and the town as you approach the bridge into Dent.

.Trail No 3

(Dent, Deepdale, Kingdale, Ingleton, Chapel Le Dale, Newby Head, Cowgill, Dent).

Approx 27 miles.

*T*his is a short but hilly trail. The easiest way "round" is to climb up Deepdale out of Dent and down Kingdale to Ingleton. You should then, with a bit of luck, only have to walk up Deepdale! On a nice day flanked by the massive Whernside on your left, this is no problem. Keep looking behind you for the wonderful views of Dentdale and surrounding countryside. You can start this trail from Dent or from Ingleton. Both are nice places to start and to finish a trail. I've given the directions from Ingleton.

Popular Dales Walk

Ingleton has many happy memories for me. My first cycling club, The Bradford Racing Club used to spend every "plot" night, November 5th, in Ingleton. We either stayed at the Youth Hostel, which is in the main street, or bed and breakfast.

Our favourite haunt was the Wheatsheaf Hotel. It was handy for the Youth Hostel, just across the road, or for the dance. The latter was always a riot! Not literally in those days, although it could have been!

You went up a flight of "outside" stairs to the dance. At the top you paid your shilling or whatever, and had the back of your hand stamped with a rubber stamp. You were now free to come and go! Going meant a visit to the Wheatsheaf to get the necessary courage to ask one of the lasses for a dance!

Saturday night it was full of local lads and lasses, cyclists, hikers and the occasional police man. The police station is just up the street. There was a small band, bare wood boards, and a lot of enthusiasm. Not a lot of top class ball room dancing going on, but then, that's not what we were there for!

There was also a small cinema and, as today, plenty of good cafes. It's worth spending some time in Ingleton whether you start from here or from Dent. White Scar Cavern is within walking distance and has spectacular displays of stalactites and stalagmites. One of the most scenic and picturesque walks in the Dales, a walk to Ingleton Falls, starts in the car park here.

The Three Peaks

You can start in the centre of Ingleton and make your way up through the main street. This takes you out of the town and onto the B6255 heading for Hawes. I have always liked climbing out of Ingleton on this road. As you leave the town the open and inviting countryside seems to open up before you.

Once over this first short but steep bit there are no more serious climbs until you reach Dent 18 miles away. On a nice day this is one of my favourite stretches of road. The steadily rising bulk of Ingleborough on your right and the start of Whernside on your left. Just a few more miles and you will get your first view of Pen-y-ghent. It's amazing to think that they cycle up and down all three of these mountains, in less than three hours, in the Three Peaks race!

Three Peaks Country

My Name Is Alice White

*Y*ou're 4 miles now from Chapel le Dale. The road rises and falls gradually as it follows the gently flowing river Doe below you, and to your left. It always seems to me to be an aptly named river. The surprisingly rich meadow land of its course contrasts strongly with the rugged hills around it.

The church of St. Leonard is in the village of Chapel -Le -Dale. In it you will find a marble plaque dedicated to the many men, women and children who died in the construction of the Settle & Carlisle Railway in the nineteenth century. Two hundred of them are buried in this churchyard alone. These were some of the toughest people this land has ever produced.

The story of one woman who "followed" the navvies is told in the song Alice White, written by Alan Bell. Part of the last verse goes, *"and now I'm getting old and grey before my time, with the work and the child bearing, as I've tramped from line to line".*

Tough people, tough times.

From Chapel -Le - Dale you continue on the B6255 to Ribblehead a couple of miles away. Nothing much there, a pub and a few railway cottages, but look towards Whernside. Seeking to outdo the bulk of the mountain is the Settle & Carlisle railway viaduct. Twenty four arches and 160 feet high. This was the costliest section of the line to build as it also includes Blea Moor Tunnel. If you are in the area long enough do take a trip up and down the line. There is a continuous fight to keep the line open and the views are spectacular from the train it would be a tradegy to lose this route.

Female Solutions To A Delicate Problem!

J stayed bed and breakfast at Ribblehead pub in the late 1950s. Believe it or not, in those days there were no beer pumps. When you needed a refill the landlord lifted a trap door, descended into the cellar with a metal pitcher, and refilled your empty glass from it! Then when he thought about it, he would charge you for a pint! You were also given a lighted candle in a holder to go to bed with. There being no electricity.

It's different today! I was in there a couple of years ago with some of the Pennine club. We were camping down at Cowgill in Dentdale and had driven up for a night out. Electric beer pumps, darts, juke boxes, pool, good food , good company , the lot!

There was Cyril, Gordon, his sister Sylvia, me and Gordon's dog Keld in the car going back to Cowgill. We'd all had a few, except Gordon who was driving, and our senses were somewhat dulled. But Keld had a nasty habit of rolling his eyes,looking at you all sadly, and then letting go the most deadly but silent fart you can imagine!

There were various suggestions as to what to do. Gordon, who loved the dog, was not able to accept the most obvious ones! I think my suggestion was to point him the "wrong" way out of an open window. It was left to Sylvia to come up with the solution. Thinking about it, she had the strongest motive, as the dog was sat on her knee! She opened her handbag, took out an expensive perfume and sprayed him in the appropriate area!

As you pass down through the common land of Ribblehead, look out for views of Pen-Y-Ghent on your right. The road starts to rise and you are soon passing what looks to be an old farm. This is Gearstones. It has in my time been a cafe, but in the days of the cattle drovers, it was an overnight resting place. In Sir William Addison's book, "The Old Roads of England", it is described in 1792 as being, "the seat of misery, yet crammed with Scots cattle dealers in plaids and kilts, the heath in front of it thronged with Scots cattle and drovers". It's a bit quieter now!

You climb very steadily as the road twists and turns following the course of Gayle Beck. There are always a lot of notices asking you to look out for lambs on this stretch. As you almost reach the summit of the climb, watch out for the little road on your left. This is signposted Dent 7 miles. You take this road which is close to the Pennine Way on your left.

The first half mile is flat, do make sure your brakes are working OK on this stretch. As the road opens up you start to descend rapidly towards Dent Head Viaduct. This is a popular spot for Settle - Carlisle train spotters. If a "steam " train is due there may be 50 or more lurking about! So watch out as they are likely to charge across the road en mass for a better view. It's not always easy to stop on a bike down here.

Below the viaduct the road follows the course of the Dee as it bubbles over rocky ledges. Past the Youth Hostel on your left to the bridge. Be careful on this bridge, it is narrow. There are plenty of deep gouges where lorries and buses have scraped it. Another 100 yards and you are passing the famous Sportsman Inn. I've spent a lot of happy hours in there! Often being led astray by my kids!

After you have passed The Sportsman the next large camping field is John Irvin's at Cowgill. I've walked this stretch of road on many a clear moonlit night on the way back to my tent from the Sportsman. If I ever wandered across the road a little, I blamed Gordon's dog Keld for leading me off!

After you have passed the church at Cowgill, immediately on your left is a bridge. You can, if you wish, cross over and return towards Dent on this road which is on the West side of the river. The advantage would be if you don't want to visit Dent, then you would take the left turn a mile before Dent, and start up Deepdale on your return to Ingleton.

I'll assume you have passed the bridge and are carrying on to Dent on the East side of the river. It's less than three miles of gently climbing narrow road. The last half mile descends to the bridge just outside the town. Once over the bridge you enter Dent on a cobbled street with the church on the right and some shops on your left.

You swing left at the George and Dragon Hotel. This was a temperance hotel when I first cycled here with The Bradford Racing Club in 1949. Not anymore ! Now like its sister pub The Sun it is one of the main centres of the community. Most times in the summer it will be full of hikers, cyclists, locals, and family groups of visitors. The beer is good as well. One of the beers called "Rams Bottom", is brewed in Dent's own brewery! I said there was a lot to know about Dent.

Continue on the cobbled section past the Post Office to where you swing left and start heading out of Dent. You're about 10 miles now from Ingleton and the end of this trail. You climb up past the outdoor centre on your right. After just over half a mile you will come to the right turn that takes you up Deepdale.

This is one of my favourite ascents. It's about 4 miles long and steep in places and there are three gates to negotiate but the views all around are wonderful. So ride where you can and walk where you must!

You may hit a potential problem on the bottom stretch. The road all the way up is narrow but especially so at the bottom. There are also hedges on both sides and these can be the problem. The hedges are cut with flailing chains. This process throws thorns all over the place, and can cause punctures, so watch out.

As you approach the top it can be a little frustrating as there are a couple of "false" summits. You think you're at the top, then the road dips and starts to climb again! Once over the top it's 6 miles of more or less steady descending through the waiting Kingdale to Ingleton!

Do You Like Children?

*K*ingdale is an almost forgotten dale. It's a lonely dale with only a couple of farms and I don't think any other dwellings. It takes its name from one of the Kings of the vikings called Yorda. He was a giant and would have answered the question "do you like children?" with "yum, yum yes please!"

His home was a large cave and is still there of course. His "diet" was small children, and he had a preference for eating boys, I suppose you do get a little bit more! Yorda's cave is near the top of Kingdale and is easy to find if you want to have a look at it. If you decide to go in be careful, as in the inner chamber is a large waterfall! As you can imagine it can be a little damp!

As you start to approach the foot of the dale you get a series of contrasting colours and features. Kingdale beck itself wandering along through green meadow land. Contrasting with the near white to dirty grey of the limestone crags all around.

You climb a little before dropping down into Thornton in Lonsdale. It's a lovely village and typical of so many in that the two key features are the church Saint Oswald's, and the Morton Arms Inn. I suppose the church will be the oldest but the Inn has been there since 1679! It has quite a reputation for its beers, 15 different kinds at the last count!

You have just a short distance now to Ingleton. Under the old railway bridge, over the river Greta, and you're back in Ingleton.

I hope you enjoyed this trail. I've done it many times and look forward to doing it a few more times yet!

LAKELAND TRAILS

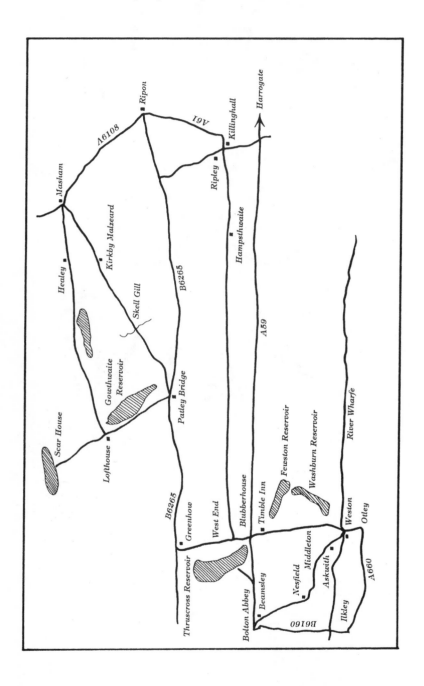

The Lake Land Trail (Well, Reservoirs Anyway)

(Otley, Ilkley, Bolton Abbey, Blubberhouses, Pateley Bridge, Ripon, Ripley, Lofthouse, Kirby Mailzard)

The first trail is quite flat, but once you go up into Nidderdale the hills are severe. On the bad ones walk and have a look round. It seems to be a case of the steeper the hill the nicer the views. Do take great care on some of the descents, I'll warn you about the worst.

Trail 1 - Otley, Ilkley, Bolton Abbey, West End, Bluberhouses Otley.

(30.miles approx)

Otley Market

J suggest that you start your ride in the Otley market square. There's a small clock tower and some covered- in wooden seats that are actually part of the market, held three days a week. The clock Tower is worth a look at. It says that it was presented by grateful Belgium refugees in 1915.

Cyclists have gathered here for donkey's years. Both before setting off on a Sunday morning and to meet up at night before going home. This was before T.V!

Happy Souls

*T*here were some underground toilets in the square. On a Sunday night, looking back it always seemed to be winter and raining, the Salvation Army band would be playing. Most of the cycling clubs from Bradford and Leeds would be stood round chatting about the day's ride.

I don't remember us joining in with the singing much, but we always joined in with the chorus of "Happy Souls", singing "Are p..s oles, Are p..s oles", at the tops of our voices.! Happy days.

P.o.w. Camps And Toll Bridges

*L*eave the market square, through the traffic lights and past the statue of Thomas Chippendale. The famous furniture maker of the eighteenth century. He was christened in the parish church in 1718. Go over the river, start to climb Bilhams Hill for Blubber-houses, and take your first left on Weston Lane, and you're heading for Ilkley. You soon pass Tetley's (the brewers) training establishment on your left. Fancy having a training establishment for drinking beer, I taught myself!

Straight ahead there are lovely views of the Wharfe Valley. After about a mile, you come to the first sharp little hill. Just right to get the lungs going. The next stop is the village of Askham. Just before you get to Askham I'm sure there used to be a camp for

Italian prisoners of war, but there's no sign of it now. In the village itself, we again pass a sign for Blubberhouses (4 and a half miles), that will be on your right but keep straight on, down the short hill and over the bridge.

The road now takes you for two miles ,through very lush grazing land, with just a few trees here and there. You're close to the river and the first bridge you pass on your left, I seem to remember when it was a toll bridge! But if I'm right, that's some time ago.

Bluebells And Crayfishing

You're just a mile from Ilkley now and Middleton is to your right. As you head for Ilkley, you'll pass some stepping stones on the river. If a group are crossing over it's always worth stopping on the odd chance someone falls in! They often do.

This is a nice area. The Middleton woods on your right are a mass of bluebells in the spring. The river at this spot had, at one time, a secret. crayfish; I fished for them here and only found out later that the location of crayfish is kept a secret by the locals.

They will be even rarer now. I saw a Country-File programme on T.V. that said imported North American crayfish are wiping ours out. They do this by infecting the local crayfish with a fungus that kills them.

Ilkley Moors B't At
(translated Ilkley Moors without your hat!)

You approach this little gem of a town , passing the open air swimming pool on your right(I've never seen anyone swimming yet!) They must have been tougher in Victorian times. At the next road junction we go straight across, but if you fancy a trip into Ilkley it is well worth a visit, just turn left. Behind the town you can see Ilkley Moors and the famous Whitehouse and Roman baths.

Your road is signposted Nesfield two miles. Don't panic when you see the steep hill in front of you! We turn left on Nesfield Road. This takes you past the golf course. I tried to play golf for a couple of years without a lot of success.   At the end I came to the conclusion it was ruining a good walk!

Bypasses And Brass

A couple of sharp hills take you into the sleepy little hamlet of Nesfield. Just 30 or so dwellings. The small beck is beautifully clean and tidy. I met the lady who keeps it that way as a labour of love.

She was telling me about the proposed M65 Ilkley bypass. There are four options. One of them will take it within a quarter of a mile of Nesfield. Through the heart of this part of the Wharfe valley. There are other, more environmentally friendly solutions, but as usual it looks like money and politics are winning out over environmental issues.

After Nesfield you'll find the road narrows. But this is a lovely gentle ride with views of the moors surrounding Bolton Abbey. One or two small climbs before Beamsly. After that it's half a mile to the main Skipton Road. You turn left onto this very busy road. Make your way through Bolton Abbey to the Grounds of Bolton Abbey. It's less than two miles away, but there is a new bypass being built, so make your own way by following the signs for Bolton Abbey.

Bolton Abbey

Bolton Abbey

$\mathcal{T}$here is no charge to enter the lovely Bolton Abbey estates, except for car parking. You're O.K. on your bike so follow the river upstream to the wooden bridge and the Pavillion Cafe. Guess what?, it's time for a cuppa. Try some real Yorkshire Curd Tart as well. You might want to take a walk through the lovely Strid Woods, and then make your way back to Otley for a round trip of about 28 miles. After here to complete the Trail proper, there are some hard climbs to contend with.

Feeling Peckish

$\mathcal{W}$hen the young lads I cycled with were all working, and had a bit of brass, we sometimes bought our evening meal instead of having sandwiches.

You can imagine what it must have been like. Trying to feed a dozen young men, who had probably ridden up to 90 miles that day. We usually ordered something like egg and chips, or beans on toast with tea and loads of bread. The people who owned these humble cafes were excellent, and did their best to fill us up.

One Sunday night we were in a favourite cafe in Bolton Abbey. We'd eaten everything in sight. The only thing edible left on the table were some daffodils and a bowl of sugar. I don't know who had the idea first. But someone dipped a daffodil stem in the sugar and ate it. In no time, all that was left, were daffodil heads, dropped over the top of the vase and an empty sugar basin! If you're ever really hungry, I can recommend them.

Hard And Easy Ways Across The Ford

The second part of the ride continues over the wooden bridge. On the other side, turn right for a little way to a Ford over a small stream. Unless you have "fat tyres" on I would not recommend riding across. You can however, get across carrying the bike over the large boulders. Take your shoes and socks off and wade across. Wait for a passing Friar from the Abbey to piggy back you across. Or do what I do, take the partly hidden, little footbridge to your left!

Tea-Time

Once over the stream you're onto the first of the nasty climbs I mentioned. As you walk up for about a mile there is some lovely quiet countryside to see. At the top is one of my favourite tea stops. The Back O'Th' Hill Farm. This is in the minute hamlet of Storiths. If you did not stop at the Pavillion, stop here. You will be made welcome and there are some of the tamest, and gentlest of cats and dogs for you to stroke. I always think that they must be owned by some very kind and gentle people!

From Storith you follow the road to the busy Skipton Harrogate Road. This is the worst part of the ride from a traffic point of view. Years ago this was a quiet, meandering road over to Blubber-houses. Now it's a straight,fast bypass. I find it noisy, but I feel quite safe on it. You have only four miles to do on it anyway.

What's On In The West End

*K*eep climbing for the next four miles. When you get to the summit of the hill, you will see a sign for Blubberhouse Quarries and West End. West End is signposted two and a half miles. That's your destination.

What peace as you turn off the bypass, and start to ride across peaceful, quiet moorland. You will see in the distance the twelve "golf balls" of an early warning system. The road gently winds along, over a cattle grid and through a gate. You will have some nice views of Fewston reservoir away on your right, nestling in the Washburn valley.

As you descend towards Thruscross Reservoir. Underneath the waters is, what was, West End!

At the road junction you turn right and will see a sign, Dacre 4 miles, Greenhow 6 Patley Bridge 9. You continue on this road for the next two miles back to Blubberhouses. . .

About Whales

*B*lubberhouses is a strange name for this very small community. The church of St Andrews stands all by itself at the bottom of the road to Otley. To me it is one of the most beautiful little churches in the dales. If you do stop for a look, notice the very small, but delicate stained glass windows at the front of the church.

When I was a lad, I thought Blubberhouses might have something to do with whales. But I never heard anyone speaking Welsh; Ah well.!

Mountain Bikes With Engines!

*F*rom Blubberhouses take the road for Otley, it's seven miles, 4 up and 3 down! fair enough! You will be going back through the beautiful Washburn valley. Past three of our "lakes", all situated on the river Washburn, Fewston, Swinsty, and Lindley Wood reservoirs.

Timble Inn

Most of the four miles uphill is rideable, but one or two spots are best walked. After one and a half miles you will pass the road for Timble(1 and a half miles), on your left. Timble is well worth a visit. The Timble Inn is famous with hikers, cyclists, and motor bike scramblers who charge about through the wild terrain. They are I suppose, the forerunners of todays mountain bikers.

As you start the long descent into Otley you'll pass a footpath sign post for Dob Park.

Ramsbottom Or Ewe And Cry

*Y*ou can walk up the valley of the River Washburn through Dob Park woods. We used to take the bikes through there in the winter on the annual holly run. That night in Otley market square all the saddle bags had pieces of holly tied to them.

I was once doing this walk in the spring with a young lass. We were well into Dob Park, when I noticed up on the hill top, what looked to be a small dog or something coming towards us. After awhile, I looked again, it was now very clearly a ram, and travelling at some speed! We started to run towards the gate, I knew she'd been expecting something but not this! We ran like hell and made the gate just in time.

I often wonder if the ram saw me as a rival, or was he just after another addition to his 40 brides or so!

At the top of the climb you will be level with the "Young Eiffel Tower" on the top of Norwood Edge on your left hand side. It's a radio tower I suppose. You carry on down into Otley. The road is steep so take care. Especially as you start to come into the town itself.

Otley is well worth having a look at. Just over the river, you will find a "Pavillion" type cafe. We always called this "Dunnies". There is plenty of room for the bikes outside, and the fare is cheap and cheerful!

Trail No 2
Lake Land   (starting From Blubberhouses)

(Blubberhouses, West End, Greenhow, Patley Bridge, Ripley and back to Blubberhouses.)

(approx 24 miles,)

*S*tart the ride from the foot of St Andrews parish church, (on the junction of the Otley, Skipton, Harrogate, West End roads). You can leave a car on the little road leading down to the entrance to Fewston Reservoir.

The trail is fairly hilly but mostly rideable. Most of the trail is on relatively quiet roads. The main road from Ripley back to Blubberhouses is usually busy, so we'll take a nicer route back.

From Blubberhouses you take the road for West End. It's a couple of miles of quiet roads to where you turn right and cross over the Thurcross Reservoir. It's worth getting off for a look at the reservoir, and what was, West End.

For Whom The Bell Tolls

*T*here is nothing much at West End now. Until the 60s there was a small community here with a Church etc. that was until they decided to build the Thruscross reservoir!

My sister Iris and her husband Jack, remember going to see the reservoir when it was drained to test for leaks. This was a year after it had been built, late 1960s I believe. She remembers seeing the old bridge, and the church steeple were still standing, as were some of the cottages. Even after they refilled the reservoir, you could for a long time still see the church steeple above the rising water.

I've heard it said that on a still, moonlit night, you could hear the music sounding over the water, as the old church bells were gently rocked by the lapping waves - or so they say!

At Thruscross, you turn right and follow the moor land road to the first junction . On your right and opposite you is the Stone House Inn. Turn left for Greenhow. It's about five miles of steady climbing across beautiful, heather filled moorland.

Greenhow is a little, rugged village where people have lived as a community since 1613, but have worked at lead mining from before Roman times.

As you start the very steep descent into Patley Bridge you will pass, on your right, a good example of a stone built kiln, complete with ground level flue. I would imagine that this is an old limestone kiln. Take great care as you descend into the town.

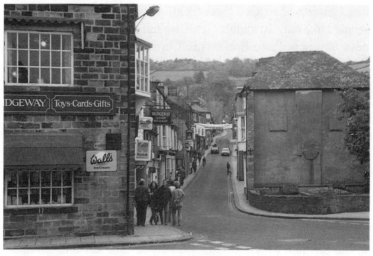

Pateley Bridge

A Golden Grimpeur That's Me!

A s you make this long steep descent into Patley Bridge think about my mate Bob Feather and me in 1988. We were foolish enough to enter what is called a Golden Grimpeur Randonnee event. This was run and organised by Audax U.K. The rules are simple. You have 12 hours to complete a route that is 200 kilometers in length and climbs TEN THOUSAND FEET. To do this we climbed the hill you're ascending six times! As well as several other noteable climbs like Par Crash, Darley Head, Dacre Bank and various lesser little treats!

It was a sweltering hot day. Bob had a severe sore throat and as we were out in the sticks most of the time, drink was a bit scarce. We finally made it to the finish in Harrogate with just minutes of the twelve hours to spare. Our first stop, still in our cycling gear was, the luxury"Crown Hotel". In we went, muck and all. They never turned a hair God bless them. Four pints of Tetleys, and it seemed like only 10 minutes later, we felt a lot better! It must have been longer because Bob's wife Christine had time to drive out from Bradford to collect us.

My favourite tea stop in Patley Bridge is at the Apothecary's Tea Rooms opposite the Tourist Office in High Street. The food and drink are excellent and you are served by charming young ladies in period costume. Give the thick, black, treacle tart a try.

A "wakeman" And Yorkshires Smallest City Ripon

Y our next stop, Ripon, is about 11 miles away. You take the B6165 signposted Harrogate It's a good climb out of the town to the junction of the B6265 where you turn left and continue climbing! well we are in Yorkshire, and I'm afraid this narrow little Nidderdale is mostly up and down.

This climb will take you up to the Half Moon Inn on your left. Looking to your right you will see the famous Brimham Rocks outlined against the sky. These strange forms, carved from the millstone grit rocks by the wind and weather over millions of years are worth a visit.

A friend of mine recently went to see a performance of Macbeth there. This was set in the midst of the rocks. The audience moved from area to area as the tale unfolded. Taking place as it did on a summers evening the atmosphere was electric.

You will pass the turn off for Summerbridge on your right. The next couple of miles take you across the top of the moor. Much steadier riding this. You're about four or five miles from Ripon now.

Watch out as the road starts to twist and descend steeply to the little narrow bridge at Grantley Hall. The road climbs up and you're a couple of miles from the entrance to Studley Hall and Fountains Abbey. These are well worth a visit. I understand they have moonlight tours of the Abbey. That must be something to experience.

Ripon Cathedral

Your last couple of miles into Ripon take you past the Cricket Club and the majestic looking Victorian Swimming Baths.

You will probably want to spend some time in Yorkshire's smallest city. The Cathedral founded by St Wilfred and made of Yorkshire millstone grit, looks dour, but is marvelous inside. One of the most interesting features of this historic building is the original crypt of St Wilfreds church.

The market square has been described by Daniel Defoe as being the most beautiful in Britain. It is certainly a busy and thriving market. If you are lucky enough to be in the square any evening at nine you will see a man wearing a tricorn hat and carrying a great curved horn. He blows this at each corner of the square. This custom is known as "setting the watch". In days gone by his job was to protect the citizens of Ripon between the setting of the watch and sunrise. Fortunately we live in much more civilised times!

There are several good cafes, so perhaps a cup of tea, before making your way back to Blubberhouses via Ripley.

You retrace the last four and a half miles on the B6265 out past the Swimming Pool and Cricket Club to the small village of Rispilth. The very pleasant well cared for countryside round here is worth a second visit.

Unfortunately, you will have the rather nasty sharp climb out of Grantley Hall to walk up! At the top you will come to Risplith. Take the first left for Ripley six and a half miles. Almost straight away you are in the little village of Sawley. Pleasant green with swings for the kids and The Sawley Arms on your right.

You're on a good road now, riding through very pleasant countryside and only one serious climb between here and Ripley. At the cross roads you turn right for Ripley, five miles. The road follows an imposing stone wall, past a converted mill on your left called the Forge.

The road takes you down over a stream and up through a wooded area called Hebden Wood. The climb is only about four hundred yards, but it's a "walker!". You will pass a sign for Brimham Rocks on your right once you are over the top.

At the cross roads for Harrogate left and Bishop Thornton right, you carry straight on. After about a mile and a half you will come to the junction with the B6165. Turn left for Ripley about three quarters of a mile away.

Your next roundabout is on the very busy A61 so approach it with care. Take the third right off the roundabout into the very impressive, stone built and picturesque village of Ripley.

French Follies?

Ripley Castle

Ripley has its own "lived" in castle. It was "remodelled" on the lines of a French village in Alsace Lorraine in 1827. There is usually a suitable cafe, but over the years these tend to open up and close down so just look round till you find one. There are also picnic tables in pleasant shaded areas if you want to eat your own food. The picnic area is by the Church of All Saints, which dates from 1400, and is in excellent repair.

Thinking about Ripley's French connection reminds me of a Randonee I have ridden in France three times, the famous Paris Roubaix. You'll find addresses of English based Randonee and Audax organisations in the address section if you fancy extending your cycling to the continent. Write to me personally, care of the publishers, if you need any further information.

The first time I rode the Paris Roubaix Randonee(literally ramble in French)was in 1984. This particular "ramble" though is 150 miles long! The event is open to cyclist throughout Europe and usually attracts six or seven thousand riders! approximately 5-600 are British. It is organised by The Velo Club De Roubaix. You start any time after 4am up till 6am and have 12 hours to complete the course. You have a "brevet", a card, that is stamped at several checkpoints usually at least two of these are secret ones. In case you fancy a short cut!

The route follows the hardest of the one day classics in the professional cycle racing calendar. It is 250 kilometers long(150 miles), but it has 40 kilometers of the worst pave,(cobbles) in Europe. It is aptly called by the riders,"The Hell of The North".

The pave is so bad, that in 1984 on one of the worst stretches I was looking at a tree up ahead. My head was being shaken about so much, the tree looked to be moving up and down and sideways at the same time!

I have seen videos of the professionals racing on the pave. In my incident with the tree I was probably doing 8 or 9 miles an hour. They race over the pave at something like 24 miles an hour!

Blubberhouses Or Bust

*E*xcept for the first two miles you miss the busy main roads and take the scenic way back to Blubberhouses, about ten miles.

Leave Ripley on the main Ripon Harrogate Road and head for Harrogate. This takes you over the river Nidd. Up the short hill into Killinghall and take the first road right by the shops. Keep going past the garage on your left and as you leave Killinghall behind, take the next right for the beautiful village of Hampsthwaite. One and a half miles.

Hampsthwaite is one of those villages that every true cyclist in the area knows of. A few miles only from major cities, it is a lovely quiet, traditional Yorkshire village. There's even an old water pump on the village green.

Head down to the Church and then cross over the narrow bridge and up the short climb on the other side. You are now heading towards a little village called Clint about one and a half miles away. Follow the signs for Birstwith just a short distance away. You are in lovely countryside and there is a nice easy descent into Birstwith over the river Nidd. At the cross roads turn right and then left at the Church of St James and climb up for about a mile and a quarter. You will pass a concrete water tower on your right. This is a lovely stretch of road, more or less straight, narrow, and quiet. You should enjoy this part of the ride. Watch out for the H.M.S Forest Moor wireless signaling station on your left. I thought it was only ancients like me that still used the word wireless. After three and a half miles you will come to the junction for Pateley Bridge 10 miles right, and Bluberhouses one mile left. Turn left of course but take care on the descent to Bluberhouses and the main Harrogate Road about one mile.

This has been a long trail if you have done it all at one go but you will have seen some varied and typical Yorkshire scenery. The tough splendour of Nidderdale in the North West and the pleasant rolling countryside further south and east.

Trail 3
(Starting From Pateley Bridge)
(Pateley Bridge, Lofthouse, Masham, Kirby Malzeard

*T*his is a relatively quiet scenic trail, but hilly in one or two sections. The odd couple of walks on a trail like this make it worth while. If you want a shorter run that avoids the hills, then I have put in a little detour from Lofthouse to Scarhouse reservoir and back to Pateley Bridge,about 16 miles. There are lots of lovely spots to picnic if you want to have a picnic.

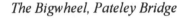

The Bigwheel, Pateley Bridge

We start from The High Street in Pateley Bridge passing the Tourist Office on your right(open April to September) and turn left at Church Street. You are now on the road to Worth although you will not see a sign saying so in the 2 or 3 miles it takes to get there. Just keep the river on your left as you climb gently up the hillside. The road is quiet and the views of Nidderdale ahead are wonderful.

You will start to drop down to Worth. In Worth cross over the river Nidd and turn right . The road will now take you up the side of Gouthwaite Reservoir. This is a nature reserve for wild birds. You follow this road now for the next 7 miles through **Ramsgill** and onto Lofthouse.

Healthy Wealthy And Stout!

*Y*ou will enter the charming little village of Lofthouse by the school. Take the right turn up past the Crown Hotel and into the green. It's worth having a look round.

The 1914 - 1918 war memorial is in the form of a water fountain. On its three sides are written the following messages of advice!

" 1 pint of cold water three times a day best way to keep Doctor away!"

"Who so thirsteth let him come hither and drink."

"If you want to be healthy wealthy and stout drink plenty of cold water inside and out."

I kid you not folks, it's there to see.

Lofthouse Fountain

Just a bit higher up and on your way out of Lofthouse on the Masham road, is a stone horse trough with the word Victory on it. It says that the **Great War** commenced and August the 4th 1914 and the peace was declared 28th, June 1919.

Before leaving Lofthouse for Masham you might like to make a detour of five or six miles to see The Scarhouse Reservoir. This is well worth a visit. Then if you don't fancy the next section of the trail, you can return to Pateley Bridge for a round trip of sixteen miles.

Detour To Scarhouse Reservoir

*B*ack by the school take the sign for Middlesmoor one mile. After a short way you will come to a Yorkshire Water sign.

Turn right along the wall past the first field to the little hut. If you're in a car this is where you pay! but there is no charge for entering the estate on a bike.

The history of Scarhouse Reservoir and its construction, 1921-1936, is shown here in the car park along with a map. It's worth spending a few minutes reading this.

The good tarmacadam, quiet road winds its way gently but steadily upwards to the reservoir. You will pass several nice picnic areas. After about half a mile look to your right and on the top of the ridge is the stark outline of a church and clock tower. There's no other indication of life up there!

On your left is the remains of the railway used to get materials to the reservoir when it was being constructed. There is still a, now blocked off, tunnel left as evidence of all the acitivity there must have been 60 years ago, in this bleak, empty valley.

Empty that is except for the then thriving village of Nidd. You pass what is left of the old village as you start to approach the top.

The reservoir itself is beautiful. The last fifty years have mellowed the massive stone dam so that now it blends into the rugged Yorkshire moorland. It seems to me to be as natural as any lake. Those who could remember it as it was are no longer with us. There is nowhere to get anything to eat although there are some toilets and a car park. It would make a pleasant spot for a picnic though before setting off back.

Scar House Reservour

Back To The Main Trail And Masham

*B*ack in Lofthouse make your way up to the water fountain and then continue straight out on the road to Masham.

Minute

*F*unny little story this but true. The climb out of Lofthouse is two miles long and the first mile is STEEP, so have a walk.

I was walking up here and looking at the wonderful views of upper Nidderdale on my left and the Gowthwaite reservoir on the right. The road is really steep and I was leaning into it, when I saw at the roadside the smallest newt or lizard, I had ever seen. No more than an inch long it was minute!,(sorry I coud not resist that one! but the story is a true one).I had not gone more than a 100 yards, when running and rolling towards me was a baby mole! I could not believe it! To see two such tiny creatures in the space of not more than 3 minutes seemed bizarre!

I wondered what to do about the little mole. It kept gaining its feet and then the slope of the hill would start it rolling again. The problem was I had no idea where it had come from. The road is so steep that it could have been rolling from the left verge to the right or vice versa. In the end I decided to let nature take its course, and hoped that its mother would find it.

After the first steep but scenic mile, the road continues to climb out onto the moors for another mile but at a much steadier rate. The top of the climb is marked by a cattle grid. With luck, you will now be in the solitude of the moors, with just the clarion call of the curlew and the harsh cry of the grouse to keep you company. The next 8 miles are mainly down hill or at worst gentle ascents so enjoy them!, as you head for Masham.

The reservoir on your right is Roundhill. This quickly disappears as we drop down to the next one, called Leighton. Be on the look out for sheep. You will want to take advantage of the downhill runs, but the sheep can be a bit skittish! In general I find that they will run away from you. When I toured the Highlands of Scotland a few years back, it was just the opposite. For some reason up there, they invariably ran straight at you! Very frustrating when you have just climbed a mountain for a couple of miles with full camping gear and then have to descend with your brakes on! I seem to remember exclaiming somewhat as I rode past them! "Get out of the way you silly creatures", or words to that effect!

You will enjoy the ride along the side of Leighton to the head of the reservoir. The road continues now to Masham 5 miles away. As you go over the river Burn just after Leighton, the road swings right. You go through the village of Healey and them shortly afterwards the village of Fearby. Both villages are well kept and the green in Fearby is a lovely example of an Old English Village Green. Just a mile and a half now to Masham. In the very imposing cobbled square is one of my favourite cafes, The Bordar

House,time for a cup of Taylor's Yorkshire Tea? Almost anyday you will be unlucky if there are not a few bikes outside.

Masham is well worth looking round. You may want to make a visit to Theakstons Brewery. They do organised tours and we pass it on our way out. If you like a pint, then I strongly recommend a pint of Theakstons Old Peculiar. It is reputed by some of its consumers to be a cure for that dreaded, "brewer's droop", induced by some other beers. I must leave you to judge (your findings in a plain brown envelope please!).

The following verse is a traditional one said by Yorkshire men when about to quaf a pint;

Oft times tha's made me pawn mi clothes,
Oft times th's turned mi friend to foes,
But now tha's here afore mi nose,
up tha pops and down tha goes!

The square is dominated by the seven foot stone pillar that was once part of a Saxon Cross. The large, mainly Norman church, with its blue clock face is also worth a visit, before we make our return trip to Pateley Bridge.

I Can See Their Feet!

Thinking about the bikes outside of the Bordar cafe reminds me of a true story. If you cycle in an area long enough, and if you are part of the local cycling club scene, then you soon get to recognise other peoples bikes. When we were lads we knew more about someone's bike than we did about them! Not only that, we were almost certainly more interested in the bike!

Bordar Cafe

I was in a cafe out near York with a pal of mine called Tommy. We were having a bite to eat in one of the two rooms used by customers, when through the window we saw another pal of ours, Malcolm Shaw, arriving on his bike. We had not arranged to meet, so he was not expecting to see us but we knew he would recognise our bikes. "Let's hide", I said to Tommy, so we hid behind some long curtains. So there we stood hiding like a couple of young lads, only we had a combined age of well over a 100!

Malcolm came in, looked round the room we were hiding in, went across to the other room, which was empty and came back again. "Have two cyclist come in" he said to the woman" who was still in the room and had seen us hide. She said nothing and started to leave. We heard him go again into the other room, heard him return and then after a long pause "I can see their feet!", he shouted.

We came out then of course and had a good laugh at his expense. Funny really because Malcolm, he's dead now, was a real practical joker himself. He was a smashing lad and enjoyed that one as much as we did.

Head'em Up Mov'em In Raw Hide

*Y*our next stop is Kirby Malzeard. Start from the square in Masham with your back to the church and looking forward to Barclays Bank in front of you. You will see the signpost for Grewelthorpe. This takes you out on Grewlethorpe Road past the Theakston Brewery Visitors Centre I mentioned. Grewelthorpe is very pleasant, easy riding three miles away.

In Grewelthorpe take the Ripon road for about a mile and then look out for a sharp right turn signalling Kirby Malzeard 2 miles. This two miles takes you through lush grasslands containing what are, even to a layman like me, pedigree cattle. That's as it should be as this was the heart of the cattle trails of the eighteenth centuary.

As you ride into the prosperous and well ordered Kirby Malzeard, it's easy to imagine it two hundred years ago. It would be more like Dodge City then! This was the heart of the drovers roads that criss crossed the country then, as cattle were driven down from Scotland as far as London. There would be thousands of cattle. Tough Scottish drovers dressed in plaid, and accompanied by numerous dogs, on their long, sometimes dangerous trail to market.

Muck Or Nettles!

*Y*ou continue through this lovely unspoilt part of Nidderdale to Laveton. Cross over the River Laver continue for about half a mile to the next junction, and turn right for Pateley Bridge about 7 miles away.

You leave the lushness of the last few miles and start out across the wild unspoilt moors. With luck the road will not be too busy. The next four miles are steady climbing until you drop down to Skell Gill. Nothing here, just a bridge over the beck, but it looks a nice little spot to explore if you have youngsters with you. Even a picnic?

Classic Dales Moorland

You climb steeply for the next hundred yards. As you level out on your right is a sign that says"Pateley Bridge 3 miles steep hill!". Put your heart back where it belongs! In reality it is a gradual ascent for a couple of miles across the moors and then a very steep descent into Pateley Bridge.

At the top of the gradual ascent you will come to a crossroads with a choice of directions. Straight forward Pateley Bridge three quarters of a mile 1 in 5! or turn left Pateley Bridge 2 miles. This is where the Yorkshire expression "muck or nettles" comes in. I go straight forward and down! but believe me it is steep! If you have any doubts about your brakes, or the strength in your hands, take the slightly longer route.

Which ever way you take you are quickly back into Pateley Bridge. It's a thriving little town with some quaint shopping areas. If you fancy a walk there are some very pleasant saunters on the side of the river.

HOWARTH TRAILS

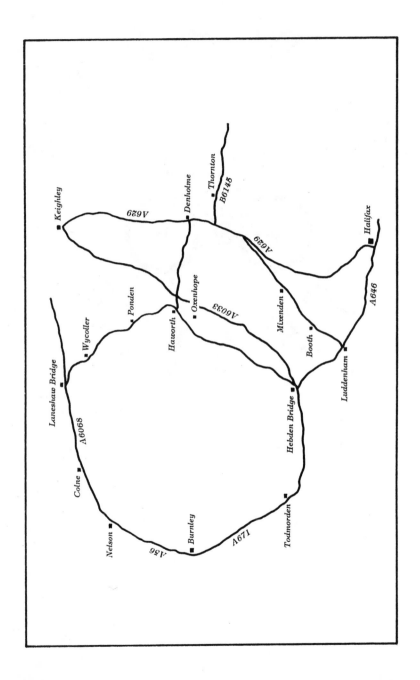

Wuthering Heights and Bronte Land
(Haworth, Thornton, Hebden Bridge, Todmorden, Burnley, Colne, Laneshaw Bridge, Whitecoller, Ponden, Haworth)

*N*ote: some of these trails are in what is still wild, open moorland. Some of the climbs are also very severe, so don't take on too much in one day. I would strongly suggest looking at an ordnance map before setting off. If you should find the rides hard there are not many return routes, other than back the way you have come. If you do the rides in late autumn or winter, please be especially careful.

I suggest that you start these trails from Haworth, outside of the Worth Valley Railway. For anyone who is a steam train enthusiast, a trip on the railway is a must. Apart from anything else, you will be following the trail of the famous"Railway Children".

Trail (1)

*Y*ou go up the hill to the Baptist church on your left, and take the left turn for Oxenhope. But you may want to turn right here and spend some time in Haworth itself. The Tourist Office (you will be part of the 2 million visitors they get every year) are very helpful and have a lot of useful local information.

After turning left for Oxenhope, take the next turn left for Hebden Bridge. This takes you down Wood House Lane, the road narrows and becomes one way as it passes the local school. At the main Denholme-Hebden Bridge road, turn right . You climb now for about two miles, with extensive views on your right of Windle Farm House reservoir. The road is usually relatively quiet, as it takes you across Oxenhope moors. You get a real sense of freedom as you ride across these wild moors.

The long, steep, descent into Hebden Bridge can be quite tricky. As you come into the tree lined part, about a mile from the bottom, watch out for slippery surfaces if it's been raining.

From Dark Satanic Mills, To Ducks And Flowers On The Canal

*W*hat a contrast Hebden Bridge is now to when I first cycled here. Then, like any woollen town ,it was smog, fog, dirt and grime! Now it's ducks on the Rochdale canal, pleasant shops, and what was always there, nice folk! This is well worth a coffee stop, and a look round.

A visit to the friendly well stocked Tourist Office confirms Hebden Bridge's long trail from Textiles to Tourists. Folk music, museums, day trips out, it's all there!

The Bone Woman

*A*bout 20 years ago, I had a nasty fall outside my home on some ice. The effect was to give me what the doctor described as a slipped disc, and agony as I drove about the country as a Sales Manager.

Having done judo competitively for 12 years, I knew all about back problems! But nothing seemed to help. At night, after a days work, I was in tears, as I dragged myself out of the car, by pulling with both hands on the car roof.

A pal of mine suggested I go and see a Mrs Few. He gave me a Todmorden telephone number, and I made an appointment. Todmorden was 30 miles from where I lived, and the thought of the drive was agony, but off I went. When I got near to the address I had, I asked the way. "Oh you want the bone woman, it's over there."

Inside of the very ordinary house, the husband and grown up son were having their tea at the kitchen table. "What's the problem?", Mrs Few asked. When I told her, she said," take your overcoat off, and lean against the wall." She then, with very little pressure, ran her hands down the backs of my legs. "That's it then" she said. I gave her the money she asked for, £1.50, and set off thinking what a mug I was, and dreading the drive home.

I could feel no pain as I got into the car, which was unusual, but I thought it's just a placebo effect caused by my mind wanting it to work. But from that day to this, over 20 years, the pain has never returned, thank God.

It may have had something to do with Todmorden itself. A recent television documentory claimed that Todmorden had the highest number of reported U.F.O.s in the country. Mind you, they also sell a lot of strong ale round here as well!

The road to Burnley opens up into an almost lakeland style, with lush meadow land on both sides surrounded by hills. This is quite a contrast to the industrialised towns we have been passing through since Hebden Bridge.

As you approach Burnley, take great care at the Skipton bye pass. This can be very busy. If it is, walk across. Your road is to the right. As you leave the junction of the bye pass, you get your first view to your left of that dark, treeless hulk,Pendle Hill. As we go for the next few miles through built up areas it is comforting to keep catching a glimpse of Pendle Hill, and to know we shall soon be out in the open country again.

You follow the signs for Briarfield and Nelson. Go past the Burnley football ground and straight on. As you approach the centre of Nelson get off the bike and walk across the pedestrian precinct. On the other side, rejoin the the road for Colne (2 miles away). This is safer than riding round by the bus station.

Your next two miles are not very interesting. The last short, sharp climb takes you up into the friendly little town of Colne.

There is a permanent covered-in market with a cafe. The street market held outside is on a Wednesday and Saturday. Should you be in need of a cuppa, I can recommend The Richmond Cafe. With your back to the Market Hall it is across the road and on your left. Can't miss it, it's in Richmond Street! There are also some handy iron posts to lock your bike to but you can see it from inside the cafe anyway.

As you leave Colne on the A6068 look out for signs for Laneshaw Bridge our next destination. It's about two miles away and you're only about ten miles from Haworth.

As you leave Colne you soon come into the countryside again. Before you come to the hospital on your left there is a short rise with a church at the bottom. Outside, silhouetted by grave stones, is a sign that says "we are a lively church", looking at the grave stones I thought "not too lively I hope!"

At Laneshaw Bridge you take the right turn for Haworth. Only a few miles now, hilly but lovely surroundings to Haworth. The road drops to a pack horse bridge and you go straight on and up, but if you have time Wycoller, about a mile away and to your right, is well worth the detour.

If you do make the detour to Wycoller you will have to come back the same way but for the extra couple of miles, I would strongly recommend it.

Albert Winstanley described Wycoller as "One of the oldest corners of Lancashire, steeped in the spell of the past, and when you gaze upon a scene that has not changed over the centuries. I envy anyone seeing Wycoller for the first time." I can only humbly echo that lovely thought.

One of its features is a "clapper bridge", the only other example that I know of is in Malham. The stone surface shows clearly the wear from the thousands of weaver's clogs that have passed over it. There is also a quaint rather scew-wiff pack horse bridge estimated to be 700 years old.

For the Bronte enthusiasts there are also the remains of Wycoller Hall, made famous by Charlotte Bronte, as Ferndean Manor in her novel -Jane Eyre.

I hope that I have convinced you that Wycoller, now part of a "country park", is well worth the extra time. It would also be a lovely spot for a picnic. Anyway, back to the main route and onwards,(and upwards!), to Haworth.

The Ancient Mariner

*A*s you walk up the hill savour the magnificent views of Pendle Hill on your right. Just before the top, you get one of the best views of this strange, bare mountain that I know of. As you pass Sheddies Reservoir on your right, you start the descent through a mass of purple heather to Ponden Reservoir.

Some years ago when my children were small. I kept a "mirror" sailing dinghy here. It was only a few miles from where we lived and we would come up as a family to sail at the weekend.

When the kids were still small we hired a small yacht on The Black Water Estuary in Essex. Not a massive boat as boats go, a couple of tons. But when all you have ever sailed is a mirror dinghy weighing about 100 lbs, and the crew is to be your wife, your daughter Catherine 5, sons Paul 9 and Simon 7, it does make it interesting!

Early in the holiday, having carefully studied a picture post card with an outline of the estuary on it, I remarked "I know these waters like the back of my hand". A few days later we were trying to find somewhere to tie up for the night. It was getting dark and I was starting to panic. The tides during the night were up to 15 knots. I did not fancy being on the end of an anchor in that sort of current.

"where the hell are we?" I said in desperation. Out of the near darkness Simon's small voice replied, "look at the back of your hand Dad!". I can tell you he is very lucky to have made 30!

Just a short distance away from the site of our happy sailing days is the old Ponden Mill. This has been in existence as a working mill since 1793. The mill closed down as a mill in 1973. It re-opened a couple of years later as a retail outlet selling top quality home linens, a craft and gift shop. It is well worth a visit when you're on the trail, so build in a little time. There is also an excellent cafe. The Weaver's Buttery, a must for a cuppa! It was in the cafe that I met a lady called Jean. She worked there when it was a working mill! My reason for seeking out Jean was to try and establish just when the mill had re-opened as a retail outlet. I think it must have been around 1976 -7.

When you leave Ponden Mill the road climbs steeply past The Silent Inn. This used to be a favourite stop in the winter for local cycling clubs. I'm afraid it looks a little more up market now. I don't think asking for a pot of tea to eat with your own sandwiches would go down well! But I have many happy memories of it. The club leaving here on a bleak winter's night. The dark, wet roads, it's always wet round here in the winter! lit only by our cycle lamps and dynamos. The dynamos would start to "sing" as we "put a mile on" to try and get warm as we made our way back to Bradford.

You're only a couple of miles from Haworth and the finish of this trail. You come into Haworth by The Tourist Office. If you're staying in the area for a few days they have a good selection of guides and some leaflets on local walks costing only a few pence.

I hope that you enjoyed this trail. Not an easy one by any means, but to me well worth the effort. I enjoyed doing it again. I hope you did.

Trail 2
(Haworth, Denholm, Thornton, Mixenden, Booth, Luddenden, Hebden Bridge, Oxenhope, Haworth)

This is a relatively short trail around 25 miles ,but it takes you into some of West Yorkshire's typical small, steep sided, little valleys. Take great care on the descents and don't be afraid to walk up some of the climbs. It is the very nature of these valleys that made them the heart of the early Woollen Industry. The steep hillsides provided the rushing streams that drove the early water wheels. Some of these small, isolated valleys would provide jobs for hundreds of people. Now the great mills are derelict in most cases.

Whirling Windmills; Saints Or Sinners!

One of the features of this trail is the Whirling Wind Generators. You see the first one as you start the climb out of Haworth. You'll see another twenty or so after Thornton.

A Haworth resident, an aggrieved one I must say, told me that the one dominating a large part of the scenery in Haworth made its owner a fortune. He claimed it produced electricity worth £13 per hour day in, day out, year in, year out! I'm sure the owner would claim it was better and cleaner to produce electricity this way. This debate will rumble on for many years I'm sure.

You leave the railway station as though you were going up into Haworth. But at the bottom of the hill going up into Haworth, you go forward and left. Straight up the steep,(aren't they all round here), Brow Hill. At the cross road ,Denholme right, Keighley left, go straight over and continue climbing Brow Hill up past the Three Sisters, I wonder who they were?, pub on your left.

Whilst you are climbing for a couple of miles, the views around are interesting. Keighley and the Aire valley on your left and moorland on your right. You will start to descend to another pub called the Flappit Inn. You turn right here for Denholme, but take great care. It's on a nasty corner of the busy A629.

Spivs From The South and Yorkshire Grit

*I*t's about two miles to Denholme now. You'll pass the Five Flaggs Hotel on your left and then start to enter Denholme passing the Black Bull.

When I worked as an apprentice in a woollen mill in Bradford Denholme was known as the "back of beyond"! It was only four or five miles away but the only transport for working people then was buses and trains. So those who made the jouney from Denholme to start work at 7.30 am, had a certain dedication. It was also common for them to walk in, and then walk back at night to save the fare! Hard people, the women as much as the men.

I worked with a man called Harris Robinson. There was no guarantee of work in those days so Harris and his wife had a small holding. This was in Denholme near the Black Bull. They ran this as well as working full time in the mill five and a half days a week. They were both in their late fifties and as hard as iron from a lifetime of toil.

Harris told a tale about the war time. In those days there was a thriving black market and a pig would be worth a fortune to an hotel in London. One day, what Harris described as "some London based spivs" arrived at his smallholding and demanded one of his pigs, or else! If you said to him "what did you do?", he looked you straight in the eye, squared his formidable shoulders and said, "ah grabbed the nearist un an brok' is leg"........! He had no more trouble with London based spivs for the rest of the war.

After you pass the Black Bull the road takes you down through the centre of Denholme. A sharp left turn and straight on, ignoring the road to Oxenhope on your right. You're heading for the Church of St Pauls straight ahead. It's only about two and a half miles from our first stop Thornton.

Where the road forks right for Halifax you go straight forward, signposted Brighouse / Bradford. The road dips and then rises. Just before the junction with the Thornton Halifax Road turn left at Keelham School. This is the quieter road into Thornton. You'll pass the White Horse and then The Ring O'Bells as you start to descend West Lane into Thornton. Down West Lane and passed the school. My three kids went to this school. At the bottom of West Lane and the junction with Market Street is The Black Horse pub.

Thornton is perhaps more the home of The Brontes than Haworth. I used to live in Thornton in the 60s. I was married in the church of St James,(the father of the Bronte sisters and Bramwell was the vicar in the mid eighteen hundreds). In those days we were aware of the Bronte connections, but nothing much was done about it. Today it has become a tourist industry led shrine to the Brontes, second only to Haworth.

The old vicarage and the birthplace of the famous Bronte children is now The Bronte Birthplace Restaurant. Outside is a plaque saying that the following members of the Bronte family were born here,

It all started here

IN THIS

HOUSE WERE BORN

THE FOLLOWING MEMBERS OF THE

BRONTE FAMILY

CHARLOTTE	1816
PATRICK BRANWELL	1817
EMILY JANE	1818
ANNE	1820

Charlotte 1816 Patrick Branwell 1817 Emily Jane 1818 Anne 1820

The poor mother! I bet she did not forget those years in a hurry!

Life Is A Series Of Ups And Downs ; Believe Me!

*Y*ou leave Thornton on the main road past The Charlotte Hotel on your left, and head for Halifax. The first two miles is a steady climb to the cross roads at the Brown Cow pub. Go straight over,A6145, to the next junction. Approaching this junction you will see about 20 wind generators in front and to your right. These are a strange sight as they appear to cartwheel across the skyline. Turn left, again signposted for Halifax A629. Up the short climb to the brow of the hill. You then start to descend past the Goose Inn, and Ogden Reservoir on your right in its setting of sombre moorland..

You pass the turning for the Halifax Golf Club onto the Sportman Inn where you turn right on Per Lane. The road winds a little and then starts to descend to a junction where you turn right. Great care here. Down the steep Mill Lane and up through the village of Mixenden on Clough Lane. The reservoir on your right is Mixenden Water. The next three quarters of a mile is a nasty climb up Balkran Road. This is a desolate little area of rundown farms, called Moor End. Keep going till you come to the Cross Roads Inn.

Straight across on Wainstalls Lane. You now start to descend a very severe hill. Watch out for the sharp left turn that takes you down towards Luddenden. Down to the bridge over the stream and climb up past the ruins of an old mill. This is a nasty little climb up past The Booth Cricket Club. The road now is flanked by several old and dilapidated mills. In years gone by they were literally a hive of industry. Now they are just a run down monument to the past.

Through Booth for three quarters of a mile and you come to a T junction. Turn left down down a steep narrow road through Luddenden to the main A646. Turn right, signposted Burnley. The next four miles take you through Mytholmroyd to Hebden Bridge. Along the side of the road is the Rochdale Canal.

As you enter the outskirts of Hebden Bridge, look out for the 6033 signposted Haworth,our next stop, and Keighley. This road takes you up out of the valley. It's very steep, but pleasant and wooded. As you leave the wooded area the road takes you through Pecket Well. The way now is not as steep but you are still a couple of miles from the top. The top of the climb,six miles in all!, is marked by the University of Bradford research centre on your right. On your left a large, brown boulder marked Oxenhope

Training Or Straining?

*Y*ou'll get some lovely views of Haworth, Keighley(in the distance), as you start the winding, mile long descent towards Oxenhope and then Haworth.

When I first cycle raced as a lad in the 50s we had an event in the winter called a Hill Climb. Simple really, find a steep hill about half a mile long or more, assemble a load of keen young men at the bottom and place a time keeper at the top. Fastest one up wins.

In those far off days we had no idea about training. The yardstick seemed to be, looking back, if it hurt it was doing you good!

One of the popular hill climbs started in Oxenhope. The attraction was probably the pub at the bottom, The Dog and Gun I think. The riders were set off at one minute intervals, so there was enough time to sink a couple of pints before you started! Imagine it, a cold winters day, a one in four half mile climb, and two pints of Timothy Taylors cold beer swilling about in your gut. God knows how any of us ever lived to tell the tale!

At the cross roads with Keighley straight forward, you turn left for Haworth about a mile away. Out on Station Road to the next junction. Hebden Bridge left, you turn right up the short sharp climb into Haworth. With one to two million visitors a year there are no shortages of cafes! So why not end this trail with a visit to one of them. Or perhaps even a beer in the famous Black Bull, former haunt of Bramwell Bronte.

Wuthering Sunset

TEA POT
TRAILS

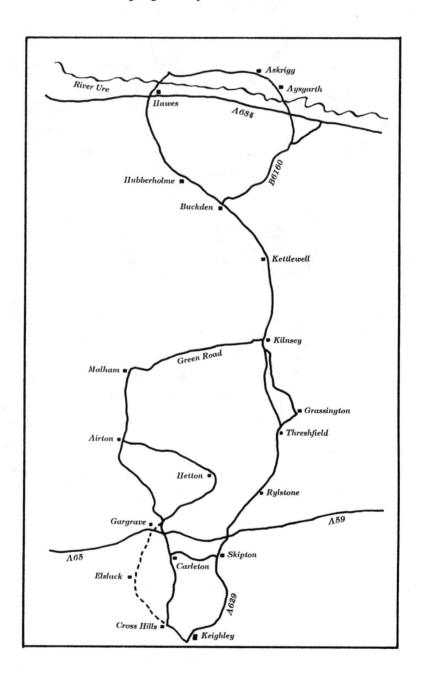

The Tea Pot Trails
(Cross Hills, Colne, Gargrave, Malham, Kilnsey, Threshfield, Skipton)

Trail 1 about 16 miles, continues onto trail 2 for about 45 miles in total.

*N*ote: There are, in the main, no severe climbs on these trails. But if you are doing the trails in the late autumn, or winter, do be careful on Mastiles Lane. If conditions are severe, then leave this trail for another day.

You can use any of the major towns on these trails as a starting point. But the directions assume a starting point of Cross Hills for trails one and two and Gargrave for trail three, and Kilnsey for trail four.

The round trip on trail one is about 45 miles, but I have broken it down into three separate circuits. I shall take us on the biggest circuit, but I will describe the places where you can turn off for a shorter ride and the points of interest on the linking route.

My First Cycle Ride

*T*his first part of the ride, from Cross Hills to Skipton, brings back a lot of memories for me, as it is the route of my very first cycle ride nearly 50 years ago. I was on my first proper bike, bought from the police lost property compound for £5 . I was with my sister Iris and her husband Jack. They were "real" club cyclists, on W.R.Bains, top of the range bikes.

We took the main A629 road from Keighley to Skipton. This is very busy now so we'll go on the back roads to Skipton on our ride.

This was my first ride, and about three miles from Skipton I was knackered! Of course as a lad of 13 I could not admit this to my older sister. She could see what was happening, and seeing a white bull in a field at the side of the road, suggested we stopped to have a look. How glad I was for that stop. Even now when I pass that spot, I still see the white bull and remember my first bike ride to Skipton.

We take the back road out of Cross Hills, starting at The Dalesway Pub which is just off the main Keighley Road. The road is signposted Colne 9 miles(A6068) and Burnley 15 miles(A56). Go up to the first traffic lights, about 150 yds. Cross over towards the Barclay's Bank, walk over the pavement, between 2 stone flower displays, get back on your bike, and head off on the road to Lothersdale. The hill is steep for 200 yds. Turn at the first right , take great care down the 1 : 7 hill. The views over Airedale as you descend are great, but watch for the bend at the bottom.

Carry on to the lovely Yorkshire stone village of Cononley. You will pass over a small stream, turn left for 100yds, then at the Institute turn right for Carleton(2.5 miles).

The road climbs and falls now, sometimes quite steeply, but all the time there are lovely views of the river Aire, and the hills around Skipton.

The Wise Geese Of Christmas Time

*A*bout a mile after Cononley, you will come to a sharp left hand bend and then find yourself climbing a short but sharp hill. At the top is a lovely, typical, Yorkshire Stone built house called of all things, Parrot Brow. Just before Parrot Brow, on your way slowly and painfully up the steep hill. There are usually a few geese in one of the fields. They make a lot of noise most of the year, but around Christmas time they seem to go very quiet! Not as daft as they look.

As you start the steep descent, on the Skipton Road, slow down and look out for the hidden left turn that will take you to Carleton. It's about a mile away.

Galloping Cows

I was once riding past here in the spring when a herd of about a 100 cows, that had been wintering inside, were let loose into the field. It's the only time in my life that I have seen cows at full gallop! What a swinging sight, talk about the Blaydon Races!

In Carleton you turn right at the Swan Inn, and you are heading for Broughton. A nice stretch of road this, it takes you very close to the river Aire, on your right side. After a couple of miles you will go over a small stone bridge.

Just after the bridge, you will come to the main A59 Road. Turn left here with care, and go for a mile to the White Bull pub on your left. Just before the pub, take up your position in the road to turn right for Gargrave. You can relax now and wind up and down some very steep but pleasant little hills. Get off and walk, it stretches the legs, and you will see a lot more.

As you descend into our first tea pot stop in Gargrave, you'll pass over the Railway Station bridge. If you're in luck, you may see a steam train on its way to Carlisle.

You can't miss the Dalesman Cafe, run for many years by Colin and Marie. Stop for a brew, I always do! The cafe will usually be full of cyclists and walkers. Drinking tea and telling stories.

One I heard is about the man who lived on his own. One bitter winters day, he could not find his cycling gloves. So being a resourceful lad, he put on a pair of oven gloves! Jennifer, a member of the same club, said she" hoped he was going to wash them before doing any more cooking." The way he looked at her, I could see this was a novel idea he would not have thought of!

Back to Cross Hills or Onwards

*F*rom Gargrave you can take the road back to the junction of the A59, by the White Bull, but this time turn right for a 100yds or so, and take the road for Elslack. This is an out of the way little village. Follow this secondary road all the way back to Cross Hills for a round trip of about 15 miles.

The Day War Broke Out

*P*erhaps the best known son of Gargrave was the comedian Rob Wilton. I don't know if the house where he was born is marked, but it was not far from the Dalesman cafe.

To continue on the main route. You leave the Dalesman Cafe by the side entrance. Facing you is an eighteenth century house, with a large imposing window. It's called the "Grouse",and was a public house up to seventeen years ago. 300 years ago, it was the local Court house, where convicted sheep rustlers were sent to York to be hung!

Next Stop Malham

*T*urn left, and take the road over the Leeds and Liverpool canal.

Turn right and join the road for Malham. This is a lovely road to be on at any time of the year. Steady climbs, and stunning views as you follow the course of the river Aire to its source. A mile before Malham, you pass through Kirby Malham. Without doubt a little gem in its own right. But overshadowed by its more famous neighbour and name sake.

Any time of the year the last mile to Malham is breathtaking. The, perhaps, most famous dales village nestles at the foot of the imposing Gordale Scar. The first pub you will pass as you enter Malham is the Buck Inn.

A lovely feature of Malham is the stream that passes through it

This is spanned at two or three places, by what are called in Yorkshire, Clapper bridges, long flagstones, resting on stone supports. On fine days, kids play on them by the hour. Cross over the top Clapper bridge, and you are outside of a cafe. Sit in one of the chairs on the grass and have a pot of tea by the stream.

Before you leave Malham, it's worth the 20 minute walk to see the massive limestone scar of Malham cove.

Limestone Pavement at Malham

An Ancient Drover's Road

*Y*ou are heading for Mastiles Lane. Take the sign for Gordale Scar, up the steep ascent to join this ancient drover's road. The "green" road is not suitable for cars, but great for cyclists and walkers. The road is bordered by dry stone walls most of the way.

This is now one of the most peaceful and quiet places in Yorkshire. But not in the early nineteenth century! Tens of thousands of cattle from Scotland would be heading for markets as far south as London. Accompanied by drovers and their dogs. All at a steady 10 / 12 miles a day! You'll meet them again at Kirby Malzaird on one of my other trails.

Fresh Baked Bread

I used to bake my own bread on a Saturday night, well what else could a Yorshire lad do without spending brass! The recipe used a gram of vitamin "C", but you only had to "prove" it once.

On the Sunday I would ride up to Mastiles Lane and have a picnic. Fresh baked bread, butter, and a flask of tea. What more could you want.

You will be on the lane for about 4 miles, and then you start the steep descent into Kilnsey.

Paying To Feed The Fishes

*K*ilnsey Crag is a limestone cliff face much loved by climbers. If you are here at the end of August you might catch the Annual Show and Sports. You will know if you have by the number of cars parked everywhere!

There is no charge to go into the excellent Kilnsey Fish Farm, although you can buy a bag of fish food to feed the young trout in pens, and it is fascinating. Children, and many adults, love this. There is also an excellent restaurant.

Or you can wander around the waters edge, watching anglers trying to catch the large, overfed trout in the manmade lakes. Not easy, they say, for the trout seem to get plenty of food.

By The Side Of The River Wharf To Grassington

*A*s you leave Kilnsey on the main road to Skipton. Take the first turn on the left singposted Conistone. You pass by a church that stands alone, the houses of the original congregation, long since gone. At the next junction turn right, and take the road to Grassington. This is Wharfedale at its best. The broad, shallow river winds its way through the wooded hills . On the road, you climb up through the woods, and then on past the cricket ground. In the spring, the banks will be full of daffodils.

In Grassington, it's time for another tea stop. Take your pick of the cafes, as you have a look at this charming village. The cobbled square now covers a stream that flows through the centre of the village.

Your next stop is Threshfield. It's just a mile away across the river Wharfe again. The descent out of Grassington is steep, so check your brakes. The road turns sharp left over the bridge at the bottom of the hill. As you pass over the bridge, you can see the natural hollows in the rocks, where people swim in the summer. A reasonable climb and you are at the junction for Skipton. We turn LEFT here, but to the right about a mile away is Longashes Caravan site.

Pot Bellied Stove And Steam Bath

Forty years ago this caravan site was just a wooden hut in a field, that sold steaming pots of tea to cyclists and hikers to drink with their sandwiches. In the middle of the hut was a large black, pot bellied stove, and on the top was a massive, black iron kettle. This was constantly on the boil. On wet winter's days the stove was covered in pairs of wet socks, jumpers, jackets, capes and whatever!..The effect was like a turkish bath. Walking in, all you could see was the top of the stove, the kettle, and the top half of people, all poking up out of the steam!

It's funny really, as now there are large mobile caravans, squash courts and saunas, on this luxury camp site/ leisure centre.

The Missing Limestone Hill

Down the hill and over the pack horse bridge that crosses Threshfield beck. Coming the other way, this has always been an exciting descent for cyclists. As you can see anything coming towards you, you go as fast as you can, and almost take off on the bridge! And freewheel up into Threshfield.

You carry on towards Skipton up a series of climbs, through wooded land until you reach the junction for Litton. Carry on towards Skipton, passing the limestone quarry on your right. As you leave the quarry behind, and start to climb towards Cracoe. Stop and Look behind. The view you see now was not there when I started cycling. What is missing is a limestone hill, millions of years old but used up in a couple of decades. The Yorkshire dales are basically limestone. How much more do we have to lose?

Duck Pond And Rylstone Cowboy

*F*rom Cracoe, it's a couple of pleasant miles to Rylstone. why not whistle or sing "I'm a ninestone toyboy looking for a woman with a car and a home and a heart of gold! "., to the Glen Cambell song Rhinestone Cowboy. Well it helps to pass the time!

Rylstone is a small hamlet, well documented in Arthur Raistrick's excellent history of the Dales, "Old Yorkshire Dales". It was reading this, that I found out that the famous duck pond was artificial and quite recent in origin.

You go past the pond, on the last four miles to Skipton. If you look up to the sky line on your left you will see a long string of sombre looking, standing stones. One day I shall have to walk up there and have a look at them. You follow the route of the "mineral railway", that was opened at the turn of the century, most of the way to Skipton. It goes from Skipton to the Swinden Limestone Quarry you passed at Cracoe.

Skipton is a thriving, active town, steeped in history. The well preserved castle that stands at the head of the town is worth visiting. The market is also worth going to. Have a wander round the back of the town, by the side of the Leeds and Liverpool canal. There are now a lot of interesting shops and cafes. Who mentioned a pot of tea! and a Yorkshire toast to go with it:

Here's health to thee an' thine, likewise to me an' mine.
 When thee an' thine cum to see me an' mine,
 me an' mine will try
an' mak thee an' thine as happy as thee an' thine med me an
 ' mine when me an' mine cum to see thee an' thine!

Leeds - Liverpool Canel at Skipton

Take the Keighley road out of Skipton that's the A629. As you start to leave the town there is a slight rise. At the top of the rise the road veers left. The hospital is on your left and on your right is a road for Carleton. Take this until you come to a fork in the road after about a mile. Take the road for Cononley and you are back on the route you set out on and only a couple of miles from Cross Hills. I suggested having the cup of tea in Skipton as there are no cafes in Cross Hills.

I hope that you have enjoyed this trail. If you have done it in one go it will have been a hard day! But you will have seen a lot of varied countryside and had a few cups of tea!

Trail No 3
(Gargrave, Airton. Hetton, and back to Gargrave about 10 miles)

This is a flat, but interesting ride through beautiful countryside, and no real hills to speak of. This is perhaps the nicest and best known part of Airedale. Our route takes us out towards Malham then swings East to bring us back through Hetton and then back to Gargrave. Gargrave is one of my favourite little spots in the dales as you may gather! My wife and I sometimes bring our caravan to the Eshton Caravan Park. There are lots of easy but interesting walks close by. And a lot of interesting tales to be heard!

The One Way Tunnel : We Hope!

I was in the Dalesman Cafe one day. It was quiet, just me, Marie the owner, and a local woman. The conversation turned to ghosts. The other woman set the scene when she described how she had been the landlady of a local pub. In the cellars below had been the stone slabs used to lay out fresh corpses before burial. She said there was also a tunnel from the cellar to the church used to transport the bodies to their final place of rest!

By this time the hair was standing up on the back of my head. She then went onto tell about an incident concerning a well known local writer. I got the impression he had died fairly recently. She, her husband and friends had been out drinking. When they got back they were all a bit tipsy. They were playing cards and talking, when the ghost of the writer appeared. I suppose if you are a ghost you expect to cause a bit of a stir when you make an appearance! But in this case they all cracked out laughing.

She then described how his face which had been pleasant and friendly, turned to one of rage! As he started to disappear; every bolt and lock in the house flew shut! I think by then they were all stone cold sober! I would have been!

The trail starts from the Eshton Caravan Park. This is just over the canal and by an animal feed merchant. It's at the end of Eshton Lane and the junction with Chew Lane.

You set out on Eshton Lane, surely one of the nicest of avenues, bordered on either side by the landscaped parkland surrounding Eshton Hall. Where the road continues straight on to Hetton and our return route, you take the fork to your left up past the imposing Eshton Hall. This graceful mansion was rebuilt by the Wilson family in the early nineteenth century.

It's only about four miles from Gargrave to Airton but surely four of the best miles on the trails. The road, whilst it is fairly narrow, is at all times interesting. You will gently climb and then descend into little shaded valleys and all the time in lush semi- wooded countryside.

Airton is a lovely unspoilt village. As far as I can see, having cycled here on and off for the last forty odd years, still largely unchanged. This is suprising really as the traffic to and from Malham is considerable in the summer.

At Airton turn right onto the village green. The green is sur- rounded by houses and must look now as it has for the last three hundred years. Mind you, I must admit the telephone wires and T.V. ariels are a bit more recent!. We are very close to the famous Pennine Way here which goes more or less in a straight line back to Gargrave and The Dalesman Cafe where the walkers can "sign in".

The road now goes down a short hill and over the young river Aire. The old mill by the Aire is now converted into flats. The Aire started just a few miles away at Malham. You go up the short hill towards Calton but you turn right on "Hall Brow". This road is marked on the ordnance as "Yorkshire Dales Cycle Way".

You meander on this narrow, sometimes twisting road to Win- terburn and then to Hetton. At Hetton you turn right and make your way back to Gargrave about 3 miles away. This road, like most of them on this trail, is ideal for cycling. Plenty of gentle ups and downs through varied and interesting scenery. About a mile before Gargrave you will drop down through Eshton Woods. It always seems to me to be a serenely peaceful spot as your bike takes you down through the woods and then over the old stone bridge spanning Eshton Beck.

Stopping The Hard Way!

$\mathcal{T}$he only problem with this stretch of road is it's a bit narrow and winding in places. A lot of years ago I was training on this road with a couple of pals of mine. Harry Starky was one and Jeff Whittam the other. We were about a mile past Hetton and heading for Gargrave.

We were all members of the Bradford Racing Cycling Club. Our main interest in racing was "Mass Start". It's when you all start together and the first one past the post wins. We used to practice a technique called "bit and bit". The idea is that you all take a short spell at the front and tow the others along. Those behind are recovering until it's their turn at the front.

We used to train Tuesday and Thursday night after work. So sometimes by this stretch of the circuit, it would be getting dark. It was dark this time. We all had good rear lights but only two front lights between us. Me and Jeff were OK but Harry was minus a front lamp.

It's a funny thing about cycling but when it's raining or starting to get dark, you seem to go faster. We were belting along. Each one imagining it was the Tour de France, and we were in the winning move with one kilometer to go!

Harry was at the front when BANG,down we went! There was not much traffic about in those days, so your main concern if you could still walk OK, was to check your bike. Would it get you home? Spin the wheels, straighten the forks, straighten the handle-bars and saddle and see if the gears still worked.

We'd done all this before the thought struck us, what had we hit? By now it was really dark. So we took one of the lights off and went forward. There, still pointing the WRONG way, if you get my meaning, was a horse! Harry said "I thought it felt a bit warm and damp!".

We stood there wondering about the horse. It did not seem too concerned at all. We were speculating what would have happened if it had kicked out, when we noticed it had a saddle on! Just then we heard a groan. So we looked over the wall and there was a young lady in riding gear just starting to stand up.

We were getting cold, which is not good when you're training. The lass seemed OK; more or less. We got her on the horse, waved goodbye and set off like hell for Bradford. Over the years I've often wondered how she got on, and how lucky we were, that the horse did not kick back when it threw her off.

If there are two or more of you on a trail together why not do "bit and bit". Every year Bob Feather and I go to the Ghent Six Day cycle race in Belgium. We cycle there via the Hull Zebrugger Ferry. We do about 250 miles in the three days it takes us to get there and back. We do "bit and bit" all the time! It's a lot safer riding single file as well. Not that it matters in Belgium, where the system of cycle tracks make it a cyclist paradise.

After you cross Eshton Bridge it's just a short return trip down Eshton Lane and you're back in Gargrave. Me, I'm off to the Dalesman Cafe for a cup of tea! And perhaps the odd ghost story!

Frozen Feet And Beards!

As long as I have been going to the The Dalesman Cafe it has never been closed except for Christmas and Boxing Day. I have ridden there on my bike on New Years Day on several occasions. It was always open.

One bitter winter's day I had ridden out to Gargrave with Bob who has a beard. It was so cold that Bob's beard had frost and ice on it! Our feet and hands were like blocks of ice!

We made it to the The Dalesman Cafe anticipating our usual tea, coffee, sausage sandwiches and sitting with our backs to the heater. For the first time ever , it was closed!

We were now too cold to get back on the bikes. So we walked the 4 miles into Skipton! God knows what we would have done if we had not found a cafe open there. But we did!

Perhaps a Yorkshire Toast as you drink your tea;

Here's to you as good as you are,
Here's to me, as bad as I am,
as bad as I am and as good as you are
I'm as good as you, as bad as I am!

I hope you enjoyed this trail. It's perhaps the easiest one in the book, but it will always be one of my favourites.

Trail 4
(Kilnsey, Buckden, Hubberholme , Hawes, Askrigg, Aysgarth, Thoralby, Buckden, Kilnsey).

(About 43 miles in total)

This trail takes you via Wharfedale into three other major dales. Longstrothdale, Wensleydale and Bishopdale. Whilst Long-stothdale and Bishopdale are sparsley populated and the roads through would normally be quieter, in the summer they will be just as busy as those in Wensleydale.

Unless you are walking there are not a lot of minor roads you can use. I have, where possible, taken a slightly longer route if it is not as busy. A lot depends on the day in the week, and the time of day, as to how much traffic you encounter. Hawes on Tuesday, market day, will be busy! But even then the fish and chips in the square are worth it!

Don't let me put you off, this is still one of the nicest of the trails, and on certain parts, even in the middle of summmer, it will be quiet and peaceful. Whatever the conditions, it's better than working!

Findings Keepings?

*S*et off from outside the Tennant Arms in Kilnsey and head out for Kettlewell 3 miles away. As you start to ride along the side of the impressive Kilnsey Crag, between you and the cliff face is one of the nicest little streams. The water is crystal clear as it travels through its limestone bed. In the spring time this meadow will be filled with buttercups and cows contentedly grazing.

Bob Feather and I were riding on here one day when we found a cow in the middle of the road! According to the marking on its right buttock it was no 246 or something. The road is narrow and car drivers tend to be distracted by Kilnsey Crag as it is without having to contend with wandering cows as well. Being perceptive sort of lads we decided that it must live round here somewhere!

We'd just passed a farm, so we started to herd the cow back towards it like a couple of sheep dogs on bikes! Once in the farmyard, the cow just stood there as we knocked on the door of the farm house. There must have been a football match on, or it might have been the farmer's birthday, because when he opened the door and we had said "is this your cow?", he just said "aye it wanders off", and shut the door!

So there we stood! Me, Bob and the cow looking at each other! There was not a lot more we could do so off we went. After a minute or so we looked back and there, sure enough, was the cow, standing in the middle of the road just where we'd found her!

Just after leaving Kilnsey the road goes more or less straight on for Arncliffe in beautifull little Littondale, but you keep to the right. Over the river Skirfare, up a short steep climb, the road swings left and you are looking towards Kettlewell. Here Wharfedale narrows into a steep sided valley. The steep, limestone crags on either side contrast with the lush meadow land on both sides of the river as it snakes its way down the valley.

Hot Air Antics

*T*he road climbs steadily until just before Kettlewell, when you drop sharply over the bridge and into the village. This has always been a favourite spot for hikers and cyclists. Over the years there have been several cafes, but perhaps the best known one was on the Buckden road opposite The Racehorses Hotel on the corner. It is still there but no longer functions as a cafe.

Some of my happiest times have been spent sat at the tables outside the cafe. A pot of tea and some home made cake or pie. Service always seemed a bit slow but the food was worth waiting for. Looking across the road to the track leading over the top of the fell to Arncliffe, there always seemed to be hikers coming down into the field, and heading for the cafe. If you were lucky and it was a calm day, there might be one of those huge hot air balloons trying to take off. If you were even luckier. The basket might tip over! All hell would break loose then as they tried to bring it back under control.

You continue on the road out of Kettlewell up the valley. The road twists turns and rolls along for the next 3 miles, through Starbotton to the last village in Wharfedale, Buckden. Besides its claim to fame as the last village in Wharfedale it also has a reputation for staging folk singing and dancing events. The Buck Inn is also worth a visit!

The Buck Inn Buckden

Just as you pass The Buck Inn, take the small road to your left for Hubberholme. The next mile to Hubberholme is very narrow and twisting but there is plenty to see as you approach Langstroth-dale. Look out for the large stone built house on your left as you near Hubberholme. A funny thing happened to me here!

When I was married in 1959 I booked the first night of our honeymoon in the George Inn in Hubberholme and confirmed it by letter. When we arrived on my scooter, we were told they had no record of my booking and the Inn was full! Charming I thought! but the person who owned the large house, hearing our story, said we could stay there that night. They even brought us a cup of tea next morning!

From Hubberholme our next stop is Hawes about 10 miles away. But first you have to climb the 1,893 feet of Fleet Moss! It's not bad really. I raced up here in The Telegraph and Argus three day cycle race in 1956. It's a steady climb right to just before the summit. You'll walk the last bit in a couple of minutes. And the views on the way up and at the top will make it all worthwhile!

Tups & Yewes

Magic Circles

*Y*ou climb quite steeply out of Hubberholme for about a mile along the south side of the river which is well below you most of the time. The road starts to level out as you come level with Yockenthwaite after a mile and a half. You can cross the river here if you want to see the bronze age stone circle on the other side. I shall always be glad that I went to see it a few years back.

At that time I was back packing the Dalesway walk. You start off at Bowness in the lakes and follow the Dalesway trail to Ilkley in Yorkshire. I was doing it with full camping gear and hoped to do the 90 odd miles in four days.

The weather was hot and I had decided to do the walk in some old running shoes rather than boots. Day one had gone O.K. I'd camped in Dent and was on target to do the walk in four days. I'd walked up to Newby Head and had come down Fleet Moss via Cam Houses. Looking at the map I had seen the stone circle, and thought it would be worth looking at.

Whether it was the running shoes or what, I don't know, but my left knee started to play up. As I came down the Moss it was getting worse. I have always found walking down hill more stressful than walking up. By the time I got to the circle I was starting to accept I might have to pack in and thumb a lift home!

It was around mid day and hot when I arrived at the circle. I was feeling despondent as I stepped into the circle. I stood in the middle, closed my eyes and just relaxed. I only stood there for a little while but as I stepped out of the circle I had a lovely feeling of peace.

What happened in the circle I do not know. But my knee no longer troubled me and I was able to complete the walk O.K. Mind over matter? I don't know.

You stay on this side of the river until Deepdale when you cross to the other side. The river is falling now in a series of natural drops in the limestone bed. There are usually people picnicking, paddling and a few camping. I'm fairly certain that camping overnight is not legal though.

The road swings North and East as you start to climb more steeply. Through desolate little Nethersgill and up to the summit another couple of miles away. The last 50 yards or so to the top are steep. Have a walk, and look out for the limestone kiln on your left. It used to be in excellent condition, but is starting to collapse as more and more people go to see it.

Be prepared for the descent to Gayle. Check your brakes as you leave the summit. After a few hundred yards the road swings to your right and then disappears! You just seem to fall over the edge, as you start to plummet down! The road also keeps dipping so you feel as though you are being pulled out of the saddle! After the first really steep bit you can relax and look around. In The Telegraph and Argus race I was told by one of the drivers of a support vehicle I had passed him down here, and he was doing over 50 miles an hour! Do take it steady.

Gayle is a quaint little place. You can cross the beck by the ford, or take the bridge. There are always plenty of ducks and geese around. Breeding geese was an important part of the local economy up to a few years ago. I read an article by Kit Calvert in which he suggested the money from the geese was the difference between eating or starving for most folk. The geese, after being sold, had their feet tarred and sanded and then were walked to Richmond I believe!

Gayle Beck

If you are O.K. for time then it would be nice to walk down to Hawes. As you leave the last of the houses in Gayle there is a flagged path across the fields to Hawes church. You may have a little trouble getting the bike through the snicket but if you can it's worth it.

There's a lot to do in Hawes. Market day is Tuesday and you are welcome to go and see the sales of cattle and sheep. Be careful about nodding your head though, you might end up with a dozen sheep! You can join the farmers in their little cafe for lunch. The food is plentiful and cheap. My other favourite eating place is the fish and chip shop at the West end of the main street.

Your road out of Hawes to Askrigg, 5 miles, takes you past the old railway station. This is now a tourist centre and folk museum. It is one of the best Folk Museums I have seen in the Dales.

Herriot Country

You cross some flat land which is often flooded so the road is raised up. At the first T junction turn right for Askrigg. This is a much quieter road than the busy A684 on the other side of the river

Ure. This is Wensleydale at its best as you make your way to Askrigg, the centre of "Herriot Country". Usually a Dale will take its name from the river that runs through it but we're in Wensleydale not Uredale!

You are heading for Aysgarth now and the famous falls about 5 miles away. When you get to the A684 go straight ahead and follow the minor road for Aysgarth. If it is not too busy the falls and old mill are worth a visit. As you would expect there is also a cafe on the way down to the falls.

You leave Aysgarth on the main road for a hundred yards or so and then take the right turn for Thoralby. Half a mile through Thoralby take the A6160. You're in Bishopdale now and the start of the Kidstones Pass route back to Buckden.

Ah Do Feel Queer!

It's 8 miles to Buckden. Whilst 6 of those miles are mainly up! I always enjoy this wild terain. When you walk the steep parts, as I always do, there is plenty to see. A couple of years ago I was walking up here with my pal Tommy. He's a few years older than me. It had been one of those memorable days. Hot and sunny with a clear sky. I know it was July as the Tour De France was on the tele at 6pm.

We had set off from Bradford through Ripon and up to Leyburn in Wensleydale. It was so hot, we were buying orange juice by the litre. We had lunch in Leyburn. Then Tommy started to complain of feeling "bad". Nothing specific, just "bad". So we sat on a wooden seat in the square in Leyburn, and after a while he felt well enough for us to set off.

By the time we were climbing Kitstone Pass, not only was he still feeling bad, his "legs" had gone as well! Charming, how do we get home? I thought. In Buckden we had another litre of orange juice and managed to limp to Kettlewell for a cup ot tea. Still 28 miles to go and Tommy moaning like a good un!

As we came out of the cafe Tommy said "is the Tour on tonight?" "Yes six o'clock" I said. He was off! Up the first hill after the bridge and it was like being in the Tour. Lungs heaving, cold tea swilling round, as I tried like hell. But no way could I keep up with him! He was home in time for the tour, I missed it! When I complained to his wife later, she just said "typical!".

Anyway! Once on the top of Kitstones if there are no cars about, it's rugged and desolate. The descent into Buckden is not too bad. You will get some nice sweeping views of Upper Wharfedale again as you level out and turn South for Buckden. Usually the Post Office does a good cup of tea. You can sit out in their little garden if it's fine. Your route back to Kilnsey is the way you came. Starbotton, Kettlewell and The Tennant Arms.

Knock Knock

*J*ust before you leave this area. Another funny thing happened to me in that cafe in Kettlewell. The one where Tommy and I had our tea on the day of the Tour De France.

I'd gone in one day for a pot of tea. The cafe inside is like the inside of an old house. You come in through the outside door and then turn straight left into the little sitting room. I've a feeling that when not used as a cafe the room you go into becomes part of the house again. If you get my meaning!

As I came through the door, out of the sunshine and into the gloom, bang! There I was, against the door, staring UP at a Rottweiler! I decided to stay still! The door into the back part of the house opened and a man came out. He pulled the dog off, and gave me a lecture about knocking before entering! He also told me the dog was only a pup at the moment(only weighing ten stone!), but it should grow to about 13 stone like its father.!

I was rather shaken by now. But in spite of everything I had my tea and then left. I was, I suppose, feeling grateful to be alive.

Half way back to Bradford the thought struck me. Who the hell knocks to enter a cafe!

I still love Kettlewell and they do some lovely buttered fruit scones at that cafe. The next time I go in though, I'll throw my cap in first. Or follow Bob and Tommy in!

This has been a long trail if you've done it all in one day. But to me this is the centre of the Yorkshire Dales. When I get to Kilnsey its like going through a gateway into wonderland. As always I hope you enjoyed it, and I wish I had been with you.

Lovely Lofthouse

GLOSSARY

Audax And Randonees

*J*f you fancy extending your cycling touring activities into the "super" league, either abroad or in the U.K., then joining organised Randonees or Audax rides is worth looking at. I have ridden several, both at home and on the continent and found them to be great fun. You will meet some of the nicest people in the world. All of them joined by a common love of cycling.

Randonee? Audax? what are we talking about? As I understand it a randonee(French for ramble), is an organised ride that you do as an individual. An Audax(French for daring), is an organised ride that you do as part of a group! That group will be comprised of men and women, from teens to seventies, riding tandems or solo machines. Whilst an Audax event is definately not a race, there is a time element involved. You have a card and this is stamped at check points throughout the course. If you complete the ride at an average speed of ten miles an hour or better, then you will receive a certificate or "brevet". I've also received medals as well on occasions.

For full details and a better explanation! why not write to:

Audax United Kingdom,
Ben Steven,
87 Belfield Road,
Accrington,
Lanc.
BB5 2JF

Cycling Magazines

There are many excellent cycling magazines on the market. Some of them will specialise in one particular aspect of cycling, for example mountain biking, whilst others are of a more general nature.

The three that I read regularly I have listed below:

Performance Cyclist,
United Leisure Magazines Ltd,
4 Selsdon Way,
London,
9ZR

Cycling World,
Andrew House,
2A Garnville Road,
Sidcup,
Kent,
DA14 4BN.

The Cyclists' Touring Club's Magazine
Cotterel House,
69 Meadrow,
Godalming,
Surrey,
GU7 3HS

Cyclist Touring Club (C.T.C.)

Britain's largest national cycling organisation, founded in 1878. It promotes recreational and utility cycling. It currently has some 38,000 members throughout the U.K. and overseas.

In addition to publishing Cycle Touring and Campaigning, the C.T.C. provides touring and technical advice, legal aid and insurance to members. It campaigns vigorously to improve facilities and opportunities for all cyclists.

It is well worth considering joining the C.T.C. if only for the magazine. This is published 6 times a year and is full of interest. It's great in the middle of winter to get a copy of the magazine sent to you showing a full colour picture of a cycling scene in spring time on the front. Makes you feel the winter is already over!

I've used most of the services offered including touring advice and insurance. The patron is Her Majesty the Queen, so you will be in good company! For more information please write to,

CTC
69 Meadrow,
Godalming,
Surrey,
GU7 3HS

Famous Cycle Manufactureres

W and R Bains. Manufacturers of bicycles from the 30s to the late 60s. Two brothers, Wilf and Reg, who I believe took over the business from their father.

Made their most famous range of "Gate leg", frames at the Eccleshill branch in Bradford, West Yorkshire. This design is still being produced today, but not by the brothers. It is sold now as the Flying Gate by Trevor Jarvis Cycles. The, then revolutionary, design enabled a racing bike to be built with a very short wheel-base. A big advantage for racing against the clock, or as it is known, time trialing.

I believe that there were three models in the famous Bains Gate range. The International, and the V.S.37 and V.S.38. The number in each case was popularly believed to relate to the wheelbase of the completed machine in inches. But I have also been told that the numbers refered to whether the frame had one or two supporting struts at the saddle stem cluster.

Walter Grieves

One of my heroes. A man who broke a world record by riding the greatest distance in a year in the hard 30s. He built cycle frames, worked as an engineer, was a local folk singer, and all this he did with only one arm! I am told that he could even change a car tyre on his own. No mean feat with two arms.

I never rode one of his machines. He built the frames "short" like the Baines brothers, but achieved this by bending the seat pillar backwards. This gave you the desired short wheelbase but also put the riders weight well over the back wheel. I am told this made them ideal for climbing. You still see them occasionally today, a member of my own club the Pennine C.C. still rides one.

I understand that Walter lost his arm in a motoring accident in the 20s. The car he was in went out of control. Walter's arm struck a metal object at the side of the road, that took it off at the elbow. He was only a young boy at this time.

The first six months of his world record attempt was unsponsored. Being a life long vegitarian, he kept going on banana sandwiches. Money was tight in those days. His mother bought the bananas at the market on a Saturday night when they were being sold off cheap.

After six months when it became obvious that he might break the record. The Three Spires Cycle Company of Coventry sponsored him.

Cycle Racing

Time Trialing

Something of a rarity in athletic endeavour. You ride against the clock, Old Father Time, not against the other people competing. The fastest person to complete the course is the winner. But beating your "personal best time" at that particular distance is just as important as winning.

All you have is your own strength, physical ability, and moral courage. At the end there is no one else to blame! The events are held on the road at distances from as short as 10 miles up to 24 hours!

Mass Start

A massed start is any race in which competitors start together, with the first man over the line the winner. They are normally held on the open roads but can be run on circuits, rather like motor racing. It is the oldest form of cycle racing but did not really start in Britain until 1942 when an event in Wolverhampton was organised by Percy Stallard that took place on the open roads.

Useful Addresses

AudaxU.K.Committee
Peter Coulsdon
UK Event Sec.
57 Hartwell Road,
Ashton,
Northampton,
NN7 2FR.

All Party Friends of Cycling,
House of Commons,
London,
SW1A OAA

Cyclists Touring Club,
Cotterel House,
69 Meadrow,
Godalming,
Surrey,
GU7 3HS.

Bronte Parsonage Museum,
Haworth.

British Cycling Federation
and British Mountain Bike Federation
36 Rockingham Road,
Kettering,
Northants,
NN16 8HG. 0536 412211

Camping Barns in North Yorkshire,
YHA Norythern Region,
PO Box 11,
Matlock,
Derbyshire,
DE4 2XA.

Dales Countryside Museum,
Station Yard,
Hawes,
Wensleydale,
North Yorkshire,
DL8 3NT.

Friends of the Earth,
26 - 28 Underwood St,
London,
N1 7JQ.

Kit Calvert's Antiquarian Bookshop,
Main Street,
Hawes,
Wensleydale.

Union des Brevets Internationaux,
120 Kings Road,
Walton on Thames,
Surrey,
KT12 2RE.
 Walton 222437

Union des Brevets Internationaux,
(France),
Alan Cordier,
BP 291 62204
Bologne,Cedex, France).

European Bike Express,
31 Baker St,
Middlesbrough,
Cleveland,
TS1 2LF.

European Cyclists Federation
C/O Friends of The Earth.
Scottish Youth Hostels,
7 Glebe Crescent,
Sterling,
FK8 2JA.

Tandem Club,
Contact(by box no only),
Box TC C/O CTC
69 Meadrow,
Godalming,
GU7 3HS.

Worth Valley Railway Preservation Society,
The Railway Station,
Haworth,
Keighley,
West Yorkshire,
BD22 8NJ

Youth Hostels Association,
Trevelyan House,
8 St. Stephens Hill,
St. Albans,
Herts.